FILMMAKERS SERIES

edited by
ANTHONY SLIDE

In Preparation:

BRIAN DE PALMA

by
Michael Bliss

FILMMAKERS, NO. 6

The Scarecrow Press, Inc.
Metuchen, N.J., & London
1983

9323986

8-92

Library of Congress Cataloging in Publication Data

Bliss, Michael, 1947-
  Brian De Palma.

  (Filmmakers ; no. 6)
  Bibliography: p.
  Includes index.
  1. De Palma, Brian. I. Title. II. Series: Film-
makers (Scarecrow Press) ; no. 6.
PN1998.A3D3373 1983   791.43'0233'0924   83-3306
ISBN 0-8108-1621-0

CONTENTS

ACKNOWLEDGMENTS

This book would not have been possible without the generous assistance of a number of individuals and film companies. I am indebted to Denny Lutz of 20th Century-Fox and Ward Abelson of Films Incorporated for the loan of prints of Phantom of the Paradise; to Steve Backer and Audio Brandon Films for their help in securing prints of Greetings, Hi, Mom, and Get to Know Your Rabbit; and to Bingham Ray of M-G-M /United Artists for publicity material on Home Movies.

Especial thanks are due to Gary Hill of Fetch Productions; and, most importantly, to Brian De Palma for his graciousness and encouragement.

All stills are from the collection of Brian De Palma; they are used with his permission.

Michael Bliss

Brian De Palma

EDITOR'S NOTE

Brian De Palma was unfairly described by one writer as "the poor man's Alfred Hitchcock." There are, naturally, obvious (as well as very subtle) references to Alfred Hitchcock's films in many of Brian De Palma's works, but such a term denies the superb, visual artistry which is so much a part of De Palma's films, notably Phantom of the Paradise, Obsession and Dressed to Kill, as well as the variant story and directorial qualities of the director's fourteen features to date. As Michael Bliss explains in his introductory chapter, each of Brian De Palma's films must be considered as separate entities; to lump Carrie and Blow Out in the same category would be tantamount to claiming that Hitchcock's Sabotage and Psycho exist on the same elemental level.

Brian De Palma is still a relatively young man, and it is, arguably, too soon to analyze his work--there is obviously much that will be original and innovative still to come. Nonetheless, this first book-length study of Brian De Palma's films through Blow Out (1981) is a welcome addition to the growing number of volumes considering the ongoing work of the new, younger bloods of the American cinema--Coppola, Scorsese and Spielberg--all of whom illustrate in their work an ability to move the art of the film forward, building a body of work of a continually, consistently high quality which will, one day, place them on the same plane currently held by Cukor, Vidor, Wyler, and the like.

Michael Bliss is an instructor of film at the University

of Minnesota. In this, his first book, he demonstrates critical skills which prove that serious film analysis is not limited to the major so-called centers of film scholarship,
namely New York and Los Angeles.

Anthony Slide

INTRODUCTION

While it may be useful for quick characterization and easy discussion, the labeling of a director as the "master" of a certain film genre can also have the unfortunate effect of obscuring the individual nuances that the director brings to his films. Brian De Palma is a case in point. Arguably since his first "horror" film, SISTERS, and most definitely since the release of DRESSED TO KILL, De Palma has been regarded as the contemporary "master of suspense," a designation reprehensible both for its meaninglessness and for its unfortunate (though doubtless intended) comparison with American films' acknowledged master of suspense, Alfred Hitchcock.

Once labeled, the "master of suspense" director is seen as a creator of shock effects and progenitor of thrills; the public is quick to seize on such a label and consequently build up expectations concerning a film's content even before the film is distributed.

The work of press agents and copy writers only strengthens the deplorable hold a label may take. Thus, SISTERS is billed as "the most genuinely frightening film since PSYCHO," an approach that blurs the distinctions between the films and plays up each film's respective murder scenes at the expense of the more subtle horrors to be derived from what may appear superficially to be the most casual and unstudied of scenes.

This book--a collection of critical essays on the films

of Brian De Palma--is intended to avoid unnecessary comparison and categorization of De Palma's films by treating each of them as an integral, self-contained text. Revealed by this method of intensive discussion is the surprising manner in which De Palma's films manage to deliver the shocks at the same time as they make significant statements about money, power, sex, politics, and the relationships among them.

It may be instructive at the outset to establish some ground rules for talking about De Palma's films. Undoubtedly, some of the most interesting and challenging contemporary writing about film is that of critics like Robin Wood and Andrew Bergman.[1] Wood and Bergman's insights into the mythic undertones of films like PSYCHO, DAWN OF THE DEAD, and the Universal horror films of the 1930s do much to increase our appreciation and understanding of these seminal works. However, as in any discipline within which a fanatical devotion to form alone is routinely applied to a diversity of films differing in their respective claims to aesthetic excellence, things can go wrong. Thus, Wood's writing about Tobe Hooper's THE TEXAS CHAINSAW MASSACRE[2] draws attention to the mythic elements in the Hooper film--details such as the use of the forbidden house, the employment of the family unit as the source of horror--without ever evaluating the manner in which these elements are employed. It should be evident that the mere incorporation of such elements does not guarantee their successful use. Yet the approach exemplified by Wood in his essay completely eliminates this factor as a consideration, with the result that MASSACRE --a poorly scripted, inartistically photographed compendium of a film that appropriates the artifacts of the essential horror film without appreciation for their meanings--emerges as a succès de'estime.

There is more to the determination of a film's significance than an assertion of its place within a tradition or its co-optation of a certain genre's building blocks. Each film must at some point stand on its own, to be evaluated as an independent unit. However, the relative successes or failures of approach and technique evident in a director's individual films can be used as departure points for evaluating similar elements in other directors' works.

To elucidate this distinction, let us briefly contrast MASSACRE with De Palma's CARRIE. Both films are concerned with outsiders; both show the protagonists (the young fivesome in MASSACRE, Carrie in the latter film) being terrorized by forces that in one sense seem external to them. Carrie returns as inevitably to the feared old house (in this case, her home) as Sally does to the home of Leatherface and family.

Both MASSACRE and CARRIE suggest that a great deal of true terror emerges from within the structure of the family unit; thus the three generations of slaughterers in MASSACRE and the manner in which the corrupt view of sexuality (sexuality being the prime source of the De Palma film's anxieties and horrors) is passed down to Carrie from her mother.

Each film presents sexual desire as a threatening undercurrent--ultimately unrealized in MASSACRE, whose corrupt family is apparently only interested in cannibalism (suggested by the repeated views of barbecuing meat--but what kind of meat?--in the film) and death; while in CARRIE, the entire movement and thrust of the film's plot is fueled by sexuality.

Yet it is clear from the first minutes of MASSACRE that the film is not concerned with its characters except as objects that may be moved from one place (the van) to a second (the old house) and finally to a third (the home of Leatherface) in order to accomplish its only appreciable purpose: to kill off (or in the case of Sally, protractedly torture) its victims. Sally's female friend in MASSACRE is more than just a young woman placed on a meat hook so that later she may be consumed; she is also a manipulated type hung on the hook of a film whose intent is to devour its victims for the meat-hungry delectation of its audience. Except for faint suggestions of quirks in Franklin's character (an avenue that is unfortunately undeveloped in the film), there is no attempt in MASSACRE at a psychological characterization of its five intended victims, who remain only objects to be eliminated.

MASSACRE's purely functional approach to plot movement and characterization is present in most of the films that critics like Wood praise as fine examples of the horror genre. The "normal" family in THE HILLS HAVE EYES, Regan in THE EXORCIST, the victims in NIGHT OF THE LIVING DEAD--none of these characters really come alive enough for the audience so that we care about them when they are threatened with death (this failing is, however, corrected in Romero's MARTIN and DAWN OF THE DEAD).

In CARRIE, just the opposite tack is taken. We see

Carrie at play with her schoolmates; sympathize with her as she is made the butt of other girls' jokes and taunts; identify with her as the frightened outsider who only wants to be a part of "the crowd." We yearn for her acceptance, are secretly thrilled when Tommy invites her to the prom and then, at the magic moment, actually seems to fall in love with her as her fragile beauty is revealed. As a consequence, when the holocaust finally rages, when all of Sue Snell's well-intentioned work turns to death and ruination, we are crestfallen along with the girl. The terrible horror of Margaret and Carrie White's deaths, and the ironic epitaph scrawled on Carrie's grave marker (an epitaph which, although it appears in Sue's twisted dream, nevertheless seems apt), are doubtless a proper reflection of the disdain in which the town and her fellows hold her, even in her death.

One is tempted to conclude that had Wood, instead of merely commenting on MASSACRE's mythic elements, devoted an entire essay to an examination of the particular manner in which it appropriates and uses such elements, his verdict on the film's validity would have been much less sanguine. It is this attention to detail, to the film as text, as integral whole, that is proposed as a critical approach here.

I am aware that a monolithic, linear approach runs the risk of ignoring insights that might be gleaned from a comparatively-based analysis. On the other hand, such a single-featured method (which departs from such a design only in drawing comparisons between De Palma films and their strongest antecedents, the works of Alfred Hitchcock) frees us to investigate more closely and evaluate the finer points of the films under discussion. Films like SISTERS and CARRIE, for example, are so marvelously infused with suggestive and symbolic meaning that it would seem difficult to do them full justice with anything less than a single-featured discussion of their filmic variables. I believe that the insights produced by my method more than justify the type of analysis employed, and establish De Palma--if such justification at this point in his career need exist--as a director whose films yield extensive pleasures at both the viewing and contemplative stages.

The Hitchcock Connection

Critics and filmgoers alike have remarked on De Palma's tendency to integrate within many of his films homages to the works of Alfred Hitchcock. The "matched doubles" (to use

Donald Spoto's phrase)[3] in PHANTOM OF THE PARADISE
(Winslow and Swan), SISTERS (Danielle/Dominique, Danielle/
Grace, Philip/Emil), CARRIE (Carrie and Margaret White,
Sue and Chris, Tommy and Billy, and the two unsympathetic
staff members: the principal [Mr. Morton] and the English
teacher [Mr. Fromm] as opposed to the understanding gym
teacher, Miss Collins), OBSESSION (Michael and Robert,
Sandra/Amy and Elizabeth), THE FURY (Sandza and Childress,
Robin and Gillian), DRESSED TO KILL (Dr. Elliott and Bobby,
Kate Miller and Liz Blake) and BLOW OUT (Jack Terri and
Burke) testify to De Palma's acknowledgment of the success
of this type of psychological characterization, the ramifica-
tions of which are discussed in the chapters on the individual
films.

In one sense, SISTERS may be read as De Palma's
reworking of PSYCHO, and OBSESSION as his derivative copy
of VERTIGO. CARRIE contains elements from PSYCHO, in
particular the emphasis on the relation between death and sexuality and the aspect of sexual rivalry between child and parent. In CARRIE's penultimate murder scene between Carrie
and Margaret White, the levitated knives that stab the mother
to death are accompanied on the soundtrack by the upstring
violin shrieks first used by Bernard Herrmann in the Hitchcock film.

Many viewers might prefer De Palma's early approach
to Hitchcock emulations, such as the playful point in PHAN-
TOM OF THE PARADISE when PSYCHO's shower scene is
first recreated--down to every camera angle and cut--and
then parodied, as Winslow uses the dagger not to stab but to
cut through the shower curtain, employing instead a toilet
plunger to secure his prey's silence. Nevertheless, in the
cases in which the Hitchcock homages appear to be essential
to the thematic development of De Palma's material, they are
discussed and evaluated; while if they are merely gratuitous
additions, they are criticized. I do not believe, though, that
there is a place for a full-scale discussion of scenes à la
Hitchcock in De Palma's work, especially since if De Palma
successfully integrates these borrowings into his films, they
in essence become his own.

More significant is the manner in which De Palma's
thematic concerns mirror those of Hitchcock. Hitchcock's
obsession with the relationship between sexuality and death
is widely in evidence in De Palma's work. As in Hitchcock,
many of De Palma's films are predominantly concerned with

investigating the aberrant behavior that arises when human beings are in the process of manipulating each other. Regardless of whether these filmic inquiries have primarily psychological (SISTERS), sexual (CARRIE, DRESSED TO KILL), or political (THE FURY, BLOW OUT) significance, it is still true that this concern of De Palma's is virtually unique among contemporary American directors.

De Palma's penchant, along with Hitchcock's, for rather dispassionately portraying the obsessions of his characters--occasionally manifested in both directors' obvious fascination with the god's-eye crane shot that blandly looks down on some of the most terrible goings on--has doubtless alienated a number of viewers, who have accused both Hitchcock and De Palma of being nothing more than showmen, tricksters enslaved to their own technical skills (such criticisms were most formidably levelled against THE BIRDS and THE FURY). It is far too easy merely to dismiss De Palma (as Hitchcock was similarly written off at various points in his career) as a purveyor of cheap thrills, a panderer to the lowest common denominator in his audience. It is quite true that those seeking vicarious pleasure in on-screen deaths and dismemberments can find ample evidence of such occurrences in the work of both men. Yet the murders in (particularly) PSYCHO (the Hitchcock murder film), SISTERS, OBSESSION, CARRIE, THE FURY, and DRESSED TO KILL are portrayed in such an obviously self-conscious, grand guignol style, and are then examined by the various detective-like characters in each film in such detail, that it is clear that Hitchcock and De Palma are less interested in thrills (the murders, after all, occupy an infinitesimal amount of the films' total running times) than in the conscious and unconscious attitudes that gave rise to them in the first place and the manner in which the audience--along with the inquiring characters--can become so deeply involved in the psychologies that they believe they are merely objectively investigating. These "detectives," it must be kept in mind, all began as observers. In this latter sense, it is clear that--like Hitchcock in REAR WINDOW, VERTIGO, and, most notably, PSYCHO--De Palma is concerned with the voyeuristic tendencies not only of his characters, but of his audience as well. De Palma's probing camera is forever observing, gazing blandly at the most outrageous of actions, while--often at the same time--the characters on screen are involved in peeking in on each others' lives (SISTERS develops this theme most fully).

De Palma will lead us up to a shocking event, drawing

out the prelude to violence with extended tracking shots, and then quickly and economically drop the surprise on us. Although Hitchcock's and De Palma's films are remarkably sparing with their violence--PSYCHO contains two murders, DRESSED TO KILL only one--the violence, when it occurs, is notoriously disturbing.

Even more upsetting than the initial murders, though, is their repetition later on in the films. After the first violent outburst, both Hitchcock and De Palma tend to slacken the pace, lulling us into a false sense of security, and then break this compact at just the right moment, usually towards the films' ends. Equally upsetting is the manner in which De Palma and Hitchcock violate our faith in the director as a silent protector of the audience's right to be only a casual, distant observer of on-screen events. The probing, tracking camera movements of these two directors become the stand-in devices for the silent observer, the role the audience traditionally likes to play. Hitchcock and De Palma, though, implicate us as guiltily in the crimes as their perpetrators; in fact, SISTERS--De Palma's extension of the Hitchcock observations on voyeurism in PSYCHO--can be read as a condemnation of dispassionate observation, which is viewed as an evil form of manipulation.

Both Hitchcock and De Palma are famous for revealing the utter depravity of which even the most apparently harmless individuals are capable: PSYCHO's Norman Bates and SHADOW OF A DOUBT's Uncle Charlie are the most obvious Hitchcock examples. In De Palma, this type is present in the milquetoast Winslow of PHANTOM OF THE PARADISE, the "mild" Dominique of SISTERS, the meek CARRIE, the at-first-innocent Gillian of THE FURY, and the law-abiding Jack Terri of BLOW OUT. That leaves DRESSED TO KILL, the film in which the supposedly trustworthy character of Doctor Robert Elliott forever breaks the good bond of doctor/patient confidentiality (in response to Kate Miller's sexual confessions) by slicing her up with a straight razor.

Like Hitchcock, De Palma is reluctant to differentiate clearly between sanity and madness, acceptable behavior and actions deemed taboo. This distinction in both De Palma's and Hitchcock's universes is so fragile that it can--at a shockingly short moment's notice--completely disappear. As Norman Bates tells Marion Crane in PSYCHO, "We all go a little mad sometimes." And Marion significantly replies,

"Yes, and sometimes just once can be quite enough. " One well-portrayed murder (and to date De Palma has given us many) is indeed enough to unsettle us forevermore, and to regard its cinematic progenitor as a man to be reckoned with.

On the following pages the reader will find discussed, in chronological order, all of Brian De Palma's commercially available films. At present, three of De Palma's early films --THE WEDDING PARTY, MURDER A LA MOD, and DIONY-SUS IN 69 (the latter a documentary of the play's presentation)--are unavailable for viewing.

NOTES

1. See, for example, The American Nightmare. Toronto: Festival of Festivals, 1979.
2. Ibid. , especially pp. 19-22.
3. Donald Spoto. The Art of Alfred Hitchcock. New York: Hopkinson and Blake, 1976.

Of De Palma's first three commercially-distributed films,
the least interesting and most banal is, somewhat paradox-
ically, the one that was produced on the largest budget and
received the widest distribution: GET TO KNOW YOUR RAB-
BIT.   Unlike its predecessors--GREETINGS and HI, MOM--
RABBIT had a tight script and worked from a unified premise:
that of an executive (Tommy Smothers) leaving his repetitive,
conformist job to light out as a "tap dancing magician, " only
to have his new life style co-opted and marketed by his former
boss (John Astin) who, for a time, ropes him back into the
same old routine of big money politics and corporate maneu-
vering that he had earlier repudiated.   Unfortunately, RAB-
BIT is overly long and uninspired; the performances of Smothers, Katherine Ross, and Orson Welles are stagy and lack-
luster, and the film's ending is woefully predictable.

It is De Palma's first two films--independently produced, comprised largely of improvisational routines, and
peppered with jump cuts, annoyingly intrusive music, and
extremely uneven performances--that are of the most interest.
GREETINGS features Robert De Niro, Gerrit Graham and
Jonathan Worden, the latter as Paul, who is about to appear
before the local selective service board for a pre-induction
interview and physical.   What there is of the film's plot is
concerned with De Niro's and Graham's efforts to have Paul
rejected by the Army.

De Palma immediately reveals his penchant for play-

1

fully using television in his films (an attribute in evidence
most strongly in SISTERS and BLOW OUT) by opening
GREETINGS with a tape of President Johnson attempting to
drum up support for the Vietnam War ("I'm not saying you
never had it so good," says the President, "but that is true,
isn't it?"). At the time that GREETINGS was released (1968)
the war was already highly unpopular with the nation's liberals
and, most importantly, with the film's intended audience: its
youth.

The trio pass from one situation to another, some
rather comical and concise, such as Paul's walking into a
working man's bar and asking, "Which of you niggers is man
enough to take me on?" so that someone, he hopes, will
break his leg for him; or Paul's attempts at computer dating
(one liaison, with a woman identified as "Ethel from Paramus,
New Jersey," is tellingly accurate in its capturing of the New
York/New Jersey Jewish princess syndrome).

On the other hand, some of these sequences are rather
repetitious and disappointing: for example, Graham's and De
Niro's attempts to keep Paul awake for three days, or their
less promising, extended attempt to have Paul pose as a
homosexual.

The most interesting thing in GREETINGS is the film's
sub-plot about Graham's fixation on the Kennedy assassination.
We have seen Paul call on a tastelessly dressed young woman
who becomes extremely offended when he asks her where she
sleeps.   ("You just wanted to know where the bed was," she
says.)   Later, this same woman, having shed her false modesty along with all of her clothes, is at Graham's mercy.
Ignoring her sexually, he traces the Kennedy entrance and
exit wounds reported by the Warren Commission on her body
to prove that the Commission misinterpreted (evidently intentionally) the evidence.   "We'll crack this case wide open,"
he keeps stating.

In the New York bookstore where he works, Graham
meets up with an extremely apprehensive man who states he
was in a Dallas rooming house which Lee Harvey Oswald
rushed into after the assassination.   The man claims to be
"victim number 17" on "the witness hit list," and tells Gra-

[Opposite:]   It will take more magic than Tommy Smothers
can summon to transform GET TO KNOW YOUR RABBIT into
a winning film.

ham that now that "he knows," he is victim number 18. Sure
enough, at GREETINGS' end, Graham is gunned down while
waiting to meet this man; his body slumps to the ground and
rolls down a concrete incline reminiscent of the grassy knoll
area near the Texas Schoolbook Depository.

It is this sub-text of violence in the film, and the
doubtless serious undercurrents involved with the death of
the Camelot/Kennedy dream in America (the crude image of
President Johnson on the television screen reminding us of
the contrast with the young President Kennedy) that make
GREETINGS more than merely the anything-for-a-laugh pastiche that it at first appears to be.

With his second feature--HI, MOM--De Palma extends
and develops many of the earlier film's concerns. De Niro
(this time resembling the Travis Bickle character from Martin Scorsese's TAXI DRIVER--right down to the delivery of
lines, the jerky hand gestures, the flashes of wry grin immediately fading into awkward stares) again stars. The concern with filmmaking and photography alluded to in GREET-
INGS here becomes the prime unifying theme of the film.

In GREETINGS, De Niro, standing outside a museum,
became involved in a discussion with Allen Garfield, who revealed that he was in reality a great pornographic filmmaker
(he actually sells De Niro a 400-foot extract from one of his
works). At this point, De Niro reveals that he, too, likes
to make movies. Shooting--either of film (with cameras) or
people (with guns)--becomes HI, MOM's overriding concern.
De Niro moves into a seedy apartment building (run by care-
taker Charles Durning in a divine send-up of scruffy landlords
leasing condemnation-prone apartments at phenomenal rates),
where he immediately sets up his camera to shoot scenes of
his neighbors' activities for a project he refers to as "peep
art."[1] With the voyeuristic theme in full swing, Allen Garfield once again enters the picture as a porn merchant, although here he is a producer (Joe Banner) who runs "The
Contemporary American Film Salon--Instant $ for Erotic
Art." Garfield becomes De Niro's backer, rather crudely
suggesting that De Niro concentrate on pure pulchritude. Referring to one of his own productions, Garfield quips at one
point, "You see that cleavage? You don't get that in a Fellini
film, you get that in a Banner film." The obsession with
breasts carries over to the Garfield character in RABBIT,
Vic, a female underwear salesman who states at one point,
"Sometime, some place, I know I can find a girl who can
appreciate a good medium-priced brassiere."

Unfortunately, De Niro's project is a failure (his camera keeps drooping down onto the tripod like a spent male
member) and his seduction of Judy (Jennifer Salt) for the
sake of his porno film is a bit crass, to say the least. But
the concern with other people's lives successfully segues into
HI, MOM's most interesting and unusual sequence: the black
theatre troupe's production of a "play" entitled Be Black, Baby.

This counterrevolutionary group (whose only apparent
white member is bearded NYU student Gerrit Graham) adver-
tises its production all over the city. At one point, Graham
and two of the troupe's members start passing out leaflets
near a subway entrance and become involved in extensive confrontations with people on the street, whom they challenge to
realize "what it's like to be black."

The startling aspect about this part of HI, MOM is
that the footage seems totally real; the people being interviewed seem unrehearsed. We thus get a melding of the
contrived (the fictional framework of HI, MOM) and the real
(the interviews) that presages the film's merger of these two
spheres in its most extraordinary sequence: the actual performance of Be Black, Baby. [2]

During this play--which is, as it turns out, a fine example of the theatre of cruelty as espoused by Artaud--the
audience is forced into confrontational situations with the
members of the troupe. The actors have painted their faces
white; the audience's faces are painted black, and the two
groups exchange roles. Politeness reigns at first, with the
traditional actors/audience separation maintained. (Later,
when the separation threatens to break down, a distraught
playgoer comments, "We came here to see a play.") But
the black actors (and Graham along with them) become in-
creasingly abusive, treating the audience like "niggers,"
calling them names, even going so far as attempting to rape
the group's most vulnerable member, a young blonde woman
who is rudely addressed as "hey you, blondie, in the green
dress."

Eventually, the theatre patrons are totally terrified.
Unable to leave the building, they are pushed into the corner of a dark hallway and are assaulted. Even the camera
person, under threats from Graham, has to step back in order to avoid trouble.

The extraordinary aspect of this extended sequence (it
lasts about twenty minutes) is that not only does what is hap-

pening on screen seem real; it seems more real than the
earlier on-the-street interviews, an effect that no doubt derives from the violence with which the sequence is permeated.
The people attending the performance do not seem like actors
(which increases significantly our sympathy for them and our
condemnation of their "oppressors," results of clear and direct manipulation of us by De Palma that tellingly demonstrate how our reactions can be controlled). None of the
events we watch seem to have been rehearsed; there is an
awful spontaneity at work here. The only sop to possible
fictional representation is the continual presence of the camera. Yet Graham undercuts this mild reassurance by continually threatening the camera operator, who is thus relegated to the party of the victims.

In this brilliant sequence, not only are the barriers
between the audience (theatre and film audience) and actors
broken down, but we completely forget the contrived nature
of HI, MOM's preceding action. The violence perpetrated
by the Be Black, Baby troupe not only confronts the theatre-
goers with the reality of the black situation, but confronts
us as filmgoers with the power of the medium to affect us
as though we were participants in what we watch. The result is that, along with Be Black, Baby's audience, we feel
threatened.

When De Niro enters the performance--in the role of
a policeman, a part he had applied for in one of HI, MOM's
earlier scenes--the merger of the real and the represented
breaks down for us somewhat since we know that, unlike the
troupe members, he is definitely playing a part. Yet De
Niro's angry, shouting cop--a man who pushes the whites up
against the wall, calls them "niggers," demands their identification, and slams his nightstick into walls, partitions and
patrons alike--reveals a terrifying capacity in the actor for
the depiction of violence-prone individuals.

Many of De Niro's mature acting gestures were already in evidence in GREETINGS. In HI, MOM, though,
TAXI DRIVER's Travis Bickle character is so strongly anticipated that we must, I believe, rethink our approach to
the Scorsese film and its "breakthrough" characterizations.
Travis is present in HI, MOM in his shouting match with the
play's patrons. In De Niro's challenging yell to one of the
whites ("What did you say? What are you gonna do about
it?") we can hear a frightening anticipation of Travis' "You
talking to me?" And when, towards HI, MOM's end, De Niro

--now a committed revolutionary--watches a public broadcast-
ing (actually National Intellectual Television or NIT, the ac-
ronym revealing De Palma's disdain for patronizing liberal
documentaries on serious issues as opposed to physical confrontations with them) show about the theatre troupe, who are
gunned down as they stage an encounter in a middle-class
apartment building, he tips the television over and shoots it
dead, an awesomely accurate precursor of the TAXI DRIVER
scene in which Travis, watching a dance show (which also involved whites and blacks), tips over his television while fon-
dling one of the deadly weapons he purchased from gun salesman Andy.

HI, MOM gives us Travis Bickle four years before he
took to the streets for his desperate vendetta against all of
the New York filth that "even the rain can't wash away." And
when, at HI, MOM's end, De Niro poses as a returned Vietnam veteran and upbraids a black psychiatrist for his smug
theorizing about why a laundromat was bombed (it was De
Niro, in the guise of a pipe-smoking proto-liberal, married
to Salt, who set off the explosion), we get a whiff of returned-
vet-with-a-grudge Bickle behind the wheel of his cab. If for
nothing else, these glimpses into the violent and reactionary
psychology of such an important fictional figure, and the manner in which the fine line between safe observer and involved
participant may be eradicated in the world of film cruelty (to
adapt Artaud's phrase), make HI, MOM a significant film,
one with which every student of filmmaking in general and
De Palma in particular should be totally familiar.

                            NOTES

1. Voyeurism--its meanings and implications--will be more
    fully explored in SISTERS, within which it takes on
    distinctly insidious overtones.
2. In an interview with Joseph Gelmis, De Palma--referring
    to HI, MOM--states, "I try to use very real people
    ... in this new film we're doing, we have a black
    militant. Not an actor. But a young kid who's radi-
    cal and who's not play acting." See also Chapter Ten
    for more on the background of HI, MOM's Be Black,
    Baby segment.

Along with CARRIE, SISTERS is De Palma's most coherent
and fully realized work.   Although it may in one sense be
viewed as the director's somewhat modified version of PSY-
CHO, the manner in which the film's story is developed, and
the incredibly insightful way in which the psychology of the
film's characters (in particular those of Danielle and Dominique) is realized, establish SISTERS as an important work
in its own right.

     It is clear that, as in PSYCHO, where Hitchcock was
so obvious about his intentional manipulation of the audience's
reactions and emotions, De Palma in SISTERS is also trans-
parently operating on our reactions.   The marvel is that both
Hitchcock and De Palma can blatantly reveal that they are
manipulating us--exposing the mechanisms they employ, even
commenting on them and eliciting a rare kind of graveyard
humor out of the deadly proceedings--and still manage so effectively to frighten the audience.

     From SISTERS' opening scene, De Palma reveals how
overt his manipulation of the audience is.   We see a disturb-
ingly tense situation portrayed.   A young black man is putting
on his pants in what appears to be a makeshift dressing room
when a young, attractive woman (apparently blind if we are to
judge from her white cane and dark glasses) enters the room.
The man stops dressing, watches the woman remove her tie
and begin to unbutton her blouse, when suddenly the camera
zooms back, a comic whistle is heard on the soundtrack, a

Dominique, through sister Danielle (Margot Kidder), returns.
The three-sided knife will soon perform the symbolic deed.

keyhole mask is superimposed over the action, and it is revealed that what we have been watching all along is a pre-
conceived scene especially constructed to work on the man's
reactions by using the woman, both of whom are appearing
on a television game show aptly titled Peeping Toms.

      The announcer's dubbing of the show as New York's
"newest and grooviest game" not only suggests that this activity is looked upon with a fair amount of approbation
("grooviest"), but also implies that the marked pleasure in
watching other people's actions has a great deal to do with
our covert manipulation of them (using them as objects of
our observation to serve our pleasure-seeking ends without
their being aware of it).

      Although Peeping Toms attempts to elevate voyeurism
to the level of an acceptable pop artifact (what was formerly
covert is broadcast for everyone to see), the insidious aspects of the activity are still intact.   Voyeurism is nurtured

by the assertion of power over others. The voyeur makes
the persons being watched his "victims" in that he observes
them without their knowledge and derives covert pleasure out
of their ignorance, laughing at their lack of control over the
situation. The admixture in Peeping Toms of awkward comedy (the audience's knee-jerk laughter in response to the pro-
gram moderator's dumb asides) and the moderator's implica-
tion that those "watching at home" are "peeping in" on things
as well, only further reinforces the notion of impotence on
the part of the observed and the assertion of power on the
part of the voyeur. One need only take one small logical
step to see how SISTERS' audience is already implicated--as
a result of guilt by association--with the audience of Peeping
Toms. There is no denying that along with the studio audience and those at home, we are secretly fascinated with the
show's mock-real situation.

     Danielle (Margot Kidder) is the "blind" girl. As the
announcer states, "She's not really blind, but that's what we
want our friend (Philip) to think." Philip (Lisle Wilson) is
thus the butt of the joke; Danielle is the partner in control.
Their date after the show may be considered as occurring as
a result of the extension of these roles, since the shared dinner is Danielle's idea. Moreover, the prizes awarded on the
show to each of the participants (as though they could somehow be recompensed for their personal shame and public degradation) affirm these roles. Danielle receives tools of power
and accomplishment (a set of cutlery) while Philip is quickly
insulted and put in his place with his gift of dining and dancing for two at The African Room, which is bedecked with ac-
coutrements of artificiality (stuffed gorillas, recorded bird
sounds) and overt symbols of Sambo-like degradation of blacks
(the waiters are dressed in grass skirts, bowlers, and white
shirts in a buffoonish yoking of primitivism and civilization).

     Virtually every piece of action and dialogue in SISTERS
is eventually seen to be highly ironic in view of later occurrences in the plot;[1] the speeches and actions assigned to Danielle, Philip, and the man in the game show audience (who
turns out to be Danielle's husband, Emil, played by William
Finley) are no exception. Danielle tells Philip outside the
restaurant that "I don't bite, that is if I'm fed I don't bite,"
although the implied quelling of her aggressive tendencies is
seen as false in light of her literally taking chunks of flesh
out of Philip with the cutlery knife the morning after she has
fed on him sexually with an appetite that (judging by the scratch
marks on Philip's back) is highly developed.

Philip's question to Danielle in the restaurant, "Do
you like to be alone?" and her answer ("Sometimes, but not
tonight") may seem to apply to her being paired off with
Philip, although after his murder one can see that the two
personalities being referred to are not Danielle and Philip,
but Danielle and the spirit of her dead Siamese twin, Dominique, who, acting through Danielle, joins the sexually rapa-
cious couple just long enough to quickly reduce their number
again to the preferred two.

In the light of later revelations, one can only smile
at Danielle's assertion that she and her sister had "such a
close bond." Given the fact that their personalities are apparently inseparable, it is thus highly ironic that it was only
after they were separated physically that the sisters' identities truly began to grow together.

One of SISTERS' endless fascinations is the manner in
which doubling (and trebling for brief moments until the un-
holy triangle is reduced to the holy couple that the dominant
personality of Dominique [Dominant] prefers) asserts itself.
As in PSYCHO--in which it was the personality of Mrs. Bates,
the murdering mother whose sexual jealousy triggered such
violent responses--so in SISTERS it is the "evil" character,
the murdering Dominique (who prefers being twinned to being
alone), whose personality is the controlling influence in the
film. Virtually everywhere one looks in SISTERS there are
doubles. Danielle's après-sex, morning-after conversation
with Dominique (a fantasy sequence that is presented unan-
nounced by any change in camera angle, cutting rhythm, or
sound, as many fantasy sequences usually are, thus plunging
us--rather unfairly and without warning--into Danielle's dualistic psychology) comes complete not only with two voices (as
in the Norman/Mrs. Bates conversations in PSYCHO) but with
the second sister's presence as well. Norman had the stuffed
and preserved body of his mother to relate to; Danielle, less
resourceful taxonomically although equally repressed sexually
and psychologically, speaks to her sister's shadow, an apt
visual realization of this spirit whose wraith-like personality
(living in shadows, in the mind's darkness of repressed evil)
comes back from the dead to live inside Danielle.

Significantly, like Norman Bates' reversion to his
mother's personality, Danielle's transformation into Dominique occurs as a result of sexual excitation.[2] Norman,
stimulated by Marion Crane (and earlier, no doubt, by the
girls he subsequently relegated to the swamp) becomes his

avenging mother to compensate for the guilt he feels over
having killed her and her lover (a lovely primal scene). Repressed sexual desire for the mother, emerging in the form
of a child's jealousy, is thus exorcised by the assumption of
the personality of the murdered "other" (becoming the other
thus surpassing sexual union by virtue of personality union).
Mrs. Bates mocks her son's courting of Marion Crane, whom
he has invited to their kitchen for a late-night snack.   "And
then what, after supper?   Music?   Whispers?"   Dominique's
statements about Philip's being on the couch the next morning
and how her sister, as a result of her desires, is "disgusting" (Mrs. Bates had referred to sexual desire as "disgusting")
demonstrate the same aversion to sexuality, the same embodi-
ment of anxiety about the sexual urges of the normal/Norman
other that are revealed in PSYCHO.

     In both PSYCHO and SISTERS, the first murders are
extremely frightening to watch.   This is not to imply that we
don't anticipate that something horrible is about to happen,
because we do.   There is a disturbing element of viciousness
in some of Norman's statements to Marion while in the parlor
(Marion: "I didn't mean it to sound uncaring" [her suggestion
that Norman have Mrs. Bates committed].   Norman: "What
do you know about caring?"); and when Marion is showering
we see, seconds before her murder, the bathroom door open
and a threatening, vague figure enter the room.   The terror
approaches in stately, measured fashion.

     Similarly, we can tell from the gradual way in which
De Palma shows us Philip carrying the knife and birthday
cake to the sleeping Danielle that something horrible is soon
to occur.   We know an awful event is at hand; the true terror emerges from the dreadful inevitability of it.   It is inevitable not only in the dramatic sense (we have reached a
point in the drama at which the underlying anxieties and ten-
sions must surface) but inevitable from the audience's point
of view, who know what the filmmaker is up to, see what is
going to happen, and are powerless--aside from the expedient
of leaving the theatre--to stop the event from being portrayed.
Thus, the horror of Marion's and Philip's murders is not only
a function of the way in which they are depicted (the innocent
shower stall becomes the place of evil; the offered birthday
cake becomes the occasion for the celebration of one's death)
but of the utter cinematic ineluctability of them.   The projection machine cannot be turned off; we are trapped voyeurs,
compelled by the moralist filmmaker to pay the price of
watching.   We are thus victimized as much as are Marion

and Philip, with the difference that the ones who torture us, placing us in powerless positions comparable to those of the soon-to-be-murdered characters, are the filmmakers themselves, who kill us with their art.

In another sense, though, the audience is far from being the innocent victim. We are, after all, rather dispassionately viewing a series of horrible events, although there is nothing we can do to prevent them. This powerlessness, unfortunately, fails to absolve us of the guilt of watching. The filmmaker thus places us in an extremely unpleasant double bind; we're damned if we look and anxious if we don't.

SISTERS' use of doubling applies to the audience as well: our voyeurism, our curiosity about the film's events (an instinct that implicitly allies us with Philip, Grace, and the soon-to-appear policemen and private detective) both draws us to, and alienates us from, the film. However, although SISTERS condemns voyeurism for various reasons, without it (as in the form of Grace's "snooping") there would have been no apprehension of the dangerously homicidal Danielle. Voyeurism is thus shown to be both immoral (invasion of privacy; cruel use of power over others) and moral (watchfulness prevents future crimes).

Hitchcock and De Palma give us visual clues that foreshadow their characters' demises, thus introducing a further fateful element into the proceedings. In Marion's case, the anxiety created during her drive to the Bates Motel is accompanied by the driving rain against her car's windshield (an aural anticipation of the water in the fatal shower) and the rhythmic, insistent movement of the car's wipers, whose annoying beat is matched by Bernard Herrmann's tense music. For Philip, the path to his death is littered with similar anticipations. The cake that he buys for the two sisters (he believes Danielle's story that her twin really exists) is inscribed at his suggestion with the words "Happy Birthday to Dominique and Danielle." The wording is an obvious attempt to appease the critical sister (and how critical she is of the previous night's actions he will soon discover) by giving her precedence over her twin. How apt this dominance is will soon be graphically demonstrated to him when Dominique takes over Danielle's body to kill him.

The inscription is applied to the cake with a pastry bag which, while being used, is shot from an angle that makes it

look like a tapering triangle (the number three appearing once
again), a shape reminiscent of the knife in Danielle's cutlery
set that we glimpsed on the game show. The same knife will
be used by Philip to cut the cake box string, and then by
Danielle to add a grisly festive touch to the birthday celebration.

The cake is then festooned with nine candles, three
for each of the three celebrants: Danielle, Dominique, and
Philip. Back at Danielle's apartment, with the cake's candles lit and the cutlery blade on the side of the plate, Philip
slowly approaches what he believes to be the sleeping form
of Danielle.

Philip leans down; Danielle/Dominique, still turned
away from Philip, grasps the knife. Philip states, "Surprise
[how much of a surprise is in store will soon be obvious to
him], you're not supposed to cut the cake until you make a
wish and blow out the candles." We can assume, judging by
her conversation with her sister, that Dominique's greatest
wish is to have Philip gone. Dominique, in a series of actions that are difficult to assimilate at one viewing (even with
the projector speed reduced by twenty-five per cent), apparently is willing to comply. The knife, on its way to Philip's
body, passes by the candles, blowing them out, and Dominique
stabs Philip three times (once for each of the celebrants),
twice in his right upper thigh (suggesting a severing of the
genital cords) and--glimpsed in a reflection on the wall in
which the Dominique shadow is again seen as she was during
her conversation with Danielle--once in the mouth, the entrance of the knife into the oral cavity suggesting a destructive sexual violation to repay last night's sexual penetration
of Danielle.

The power imbalance of Philip's sexual seduction of
the non-assertive Danielle (who was drunk, played the little
innocent, and wasn't sure at first if she wanted Philip to return to her apartment after he attempted to get her ex-husband,
Emil [William Finley] to drive away from his voyeuristic
vigil) has now been corrected. After returning to the apartment, Philip advanced on Danielle in a shot that emphasized
his power over her (the camera peered over his shoulder and
looked down at her). Redressing this sexual imbalance, the
assertive female figure, Dominique, now pays the man back
in kind.

After the initial assault, Philip starts to crawl away

from the couch, leaving a trail of blood on the floor. At
this point, mysteriously--one might almost say miraculously
given SISTERS' obvious insistence on voyeurism as a perva-
sive aspect of human relationships--the window shade flies
open and Danielle/Dominique, after twisting and turning on
the bed in what is apparently a fit of possession and pain,
finishes the job on Philip by stabbing him another three
times, this time in the back, an action once again portrayed
in a shadow on the wall.

Another voyeur, albeit of a different sort, now enters
the picture. Across the street in her apartment, Staten Is-
land newspaper reporter Grace Collier (Jennifer Salt) is about
to begin work on one of her columns.[3] Grace is the type of
writer whose overt civic-mindedness borders on a kind of
mutated voyeurism; her concern for others is so intense and
compelling that it virtually constitutes an invasion of privacy.
Grace sees through her window the final stabbing of Philip
(whether she was just absent-mindedly looking through her
window at the time or was really "peeking" is difficult to
determine), and notices Philip trying to write "help" on the
window with his blood. Despite the arrival of two detectives
whom she has called, and Grace's unknowingly accurate identification of the murderer as "someone this girl (Danielle)
knows, shorter, with a twisted face and stringy hair," the
detectives find nothing incriminating in the apartment (this
in spite of the fact that the body, having been hidden in the
couch by Emil, is already bleeding through the couch's back).
This detail, though, is revealed only by the camera/voyeur,
and is not disclosed to any of the film's characters.

We have seen that Philip was something of an impotent Uncle Tom (his acceptance of the African Room tickets
and, even more insulting, his decision to use them, as well
as his flight into the bathroom to avoid the "argument" between Danielle and Dominique suggest this). The detectives,
like Philip and the film's two other male characters (Charles
Durning's private detective--Joseph Larch--and Emil), are
revealed to be ineffective and, ultimately, useless in terms
of either solving a crime or eliminating the psychological
causes behind it. Grace, not the detectives, ferrets out the
essential clues in Danielle's apartment. It is Grace who
states that Danielle probably cleaned up the blood; who remarks on the pairs of clothes that the girl has in her closet;
who finds the cake with its dual inscription and traces it back
to its source; who visits the Life Magazine offices to research
the Blanchion twins; and who, ultimately, has revealed to her

through Emil's auto-suggestion the true psychological forces
that give rise to Danielle/Dominique's horrible actions.
Grace is subdued by the detectives (whose assertive/Kelly,
recessive/Spinetti pairing qualifies them as another pair of
matched doubles), who have her sit on the couch and keep
quiet, and tell her to stop insulting Dominique (Grace quickly
sees that the girl is putting on an act with her innocence, of
which--if we need any further clue--De Palma reminds us by
having Danielle's omnipresent gold cross flash blinding shafts
of light into the camera lens while she tries to convince
Grace that she must have imagined the whole incident).   Finally, the detectives bully Grace by threatening her with some
charge (Kelly mentions assaulting an officer--is he referring
to the cake that Grace dropped on his shoe?) if she doesn't
forget the whole matter.

        Ironically, it is precisely the film's ineffective men--
the Uncle Tom Philip, the useless policemen, the ineffectual
Larch, even (as will later be revealed) the misguided Emil--
who seem to derive the greatest pleasure from dominating
women, as though this was the only way they could effectively
assert their power, by exerting it on a "weak victim." Philip
advances, predator-like, on Danielle; the detectives bully
Grace; Larch tells Grace that she knows her business and he
knows his (detection); Emil, utterly convinced of the validity
of his analysis of Danielle/Dominique, drags Danielle to his
clinic and tries to exorcise the spirit of her demonic sister.
That all of these men are revealed to be ultimately useless
(the seducer is put in his place by being killed; the detec-
tives--as we shall see--never really solve the crime; Larch
follows up a dead-end clue; while Emil, forgetting that Dominique returns during sex, relaxes his guard while caressing
Danielle) only reaffirms the view that it is the power of the
female characters--Danielle/Dominique (and even Grace by
indirectly effecting Danielle's apprehension)--that is predomi-
nant in SISTERS.   The film's ending, which leaves Danielle
unaware of her power and Grace similarly unconscious of her
whole investigation's results, only adds a cruel, ironic twist
to SISTERS' depiction of female power, suggesting that women,

[Opposite:]   Three examples of SISTERS' view of male/female
relationships.   Top: Danielle and Emil (William Finley).
Center: Philip (Lisle Wilson) and Danielle (with her cutlery
set). Bottom: Grace (Jennifer Salt) and Larch (Charles Durning). All of the men occupy symbolically dominant positions,
attitudes they seem to prefer.

as the poor victims of men's power plays, will never be able to free themselves from manipulation and subjection.[4]

This pattern of asserted power is followed by denials of or insults to this power in the activities of Danielle and Grace. (This linkage between the two characters is firmly established in the clinic hallucination sequence, which is discussed later.) Danielle predominates over Philip, but then must seek cover under her affected meek exterior. No sooner does Grace reveal the detectives to be fools than she is picked up and degraded by her mother (who wonders when her 25-year-old daughter is going to get married and quit her "little job");[5] while private detective Larch is, as we have seen, also insulting. Yet it is while she is with her mother, and then Larch, that Grace finds important clues in the case. Mrs. Collier accompanies her daughter to the bakery where the birthday cake originated; Larch, having found the Blanchion twins' file but failing to understand its significance (when Grace refers to the file's meaning, talking about Siamese twins, Larch ignorantly replies, "I didn't see no twins up there"), was indirectly responsible for Grace's trip to <u>Life</u> Magazine and, ultimately, to the Linton Clinic (the successor twin to the Loisel Clinic where Danielle and Dominique first resided), a clinic that, in another instance of ironic foreshadowing, Grace's mother had mentioned as being a possible source for a "good story." Just how good a story we will soon discover.

It is at the Linton clinic that Grace is incarcerated by Emil, who realizes that she is aware of Philip's murder. Emil characteristically accuses the reporter of being a victim of split personality delusions; he calls her Margaret. The good doctor has previously used this dualistic trauma to exert power over Danielle/Dominique. One gets the feeling that Emil secretly welcomes Dominique's outbursts so that he can hold sway over Danielle. He wins Danielle back to him by sedating her and bringing her to the clinic; he subjects Grace to virtually the same treatment, accusing her (like Danielle) of doubling and then sedating her as well.

At this point, the ultimate confrontation with the undiluted essence of the Danielle/Dominique syndrome takes place. SISTERS has almost come full circle. The Blanchion twins, after their parents' early deaths, spent virtually all of their life together at the Loisel Clinic (where, it was revealed earlier, Emil worked). We meet the director of the clinic, Pierre Milius. In much the same manner as Simon Oakland's

psychologist during PSYCHO's last scenes provided the pat,
albeit misguided, psychological explanation for Norman's behavior, Dr. Milius in SISTERS comments on the Blanchion
Twins' case. Grace views these comments on a videotape at
Life Magazine (an interview that recurs from a reverse angle
shot during the hallucination sequence when Grace [like the
camera] is on the other side of the case--at Life she is an
observer; at the clinic, a participant). Milius states how intimately wedded and necessary the dual personality Siamese
joining is to each of the Blanchion girls. "Danielle, who is
so sweet, so responsive (we recall the scratches on Philip's
back at this juncture), so normal as opposed to her sister,
can only be so because of her sister." It is a nicely bal-
anced, pat, Jekyll-Hyde-type explanation that serves for the
present. But viewed in light of the film's end, the statement
does little to increase our understanding of the twins' psychology. Is Danielle as sweet, innocent, and responsive as
Milius would have us believe? Or is she as manipulative
and assertive in her way as her sister (and thus as danger-
ous, since her sweetness and responsiveness are the qualities that lure men to her so that her argumentative sister
may murder them)? Like the decoy that she is--ironically
she is correctly so identified by Peeping Toms' announcer--
Danielle lures men to their doom.

Is not the decoy as much to blame for murder as the
hunter? This is something that neither Milius nor Emil un-
derstands. That the former is clothed in the garb of a monk,
suggesting one whose retirement from worldly affairs involves
a lack of sophistication and knowledge, while the latter (when
we first see him in Peeping Toms' audience) looks like a repressed member of the masturbatory raincoat brigade, indicates that neither of these "authority" figures actually carries
much weight within the context of the film's communicated
meanings.

The already-mentioned hallucination sequence at the
clinic is a wonderful realization of internal psychological
states. Emil asks Grace, "You want to know our secrets?
Watch," and the camera zooms in on Grace's eye as her
voyeuristic, truth-seeking tendencies finally reveal the ultimate horror to her. She sees Emil trying to make love to
Danielle while the still-connected Dominique scowls. Danielle asks Emil, "Can't you make her go away?" and Emil
does--in this scene with an injection, later (when the sisters
are to be separated) with a scalpel. Both Emil and Danielle
would doubtless claim that Dominique's presence during their

love-making was in some sense a hindrance to them, but it
is just as plausible to assume that despite their protests,
the presence of the other--the voyeur, the watcher--excites
them. Did not Danielle take some form of pleasure on Peeping Toms in beginning to disrobe in front of Philip? To in-
vert Dr. Milius' statement, the evil sister needs the innocent
just as much as the innocent needs the other. There is, at
bottom, a strange complementarity between the watcher and
the watched.

     Grace "sees" the operation that separates Danielle and
Dominique, with the difference that as the "evil" voyeur whose
inquiries caused Danielle and Emil to flee to the clinic, and
who is now paying the price of invading their privacy by becoming the evil sister, she takes Dominique's place at Danielle's right. The fact that Grace is given this privileged
sight is quite appropriate. As a demonstrative, assertive fe-
male--one who tries to get her way despite the opposition of
oppressive men--she is very much like the Dominique personality, and is thus the correct person to share her unique point
of view. Grace's role as voyeur--the one who watches Emil
and Danielle--only further links her with the dead sister who
used to watch Emil and Danielle making love.

     The visionary version of the operation takes place in
an operating theatre replete with doubles scattered throughout
the room: two priests and two nuns (connoting the repressive, withdrawn elements with intimations of repressed sexuality and the condemnation of "lewd" behavior), and two identical male and female twins (with the Life reporter between
them, taking notes). The scalpel is a butcher knife, suggesting that in Grace's privileged view (she seems to have entered
tered totally into Dominique's personality), the operation sep-
arating the sisters was not a necessary surgical procedure,
as Emil seems to claim, but a murder. This view is actually quite appropriate. The sisters had to be separated because Danielle--pregnant with Emil's child, and having been
stabbed in the abdomen by the repressive, condemnatory
Dominique (the child as symbol of sexual union, another triumvirate that must be reduced to the requisite two)--sup-
posedly must be operated on immediately to prevent her dying of a hemorrhage (the fates reserved for Philip and Emil,
Danielle's two lovers in the film). It is not inconsistent to
maintain that Emil, tired of Dominique's interference in his
affairs (this despite the excitement of having her observe
him), desires her death: thus this dual-purpose operation,
to separate the sisters and then have one of them unfortunately die on the table. [6]

Larch, the effectively impotent private detective, blandly hands over the knife, and Emil brings it down in a butcher-like meat-cleaver chop, after which Grace starts screaming.

The nightmare is not over yet, though; the viewer now returns to the "real world." Having drugged the distraught Danielle, Emil begins making advances towards her (doubtless because of her subjugation, an aspect that excites all of SISTERS' men). He starts caressing her breast and telling her of his love, going on to explain how wonderful their marriage was until Danielle's guilt over Dominique's death became a fixation for her, so that whenever Danielle and Emil had sex, the dead sister would return through Danielle and foil their lovemaking. Apparently, Emil has not learned his lesson. Although he makes Danielle (or is it Dominique only pretending to be the innocent Danielle?) confess Philip's murder, he forgets that Dominique's return is imminent. Danielle/Dominique repeats the words describing Philip's murder ("I blew out the candles") while covertly palming a scalpel. With the same two swift strokes that began Philip's dispatch (the two strokes instead of three suggesting that at this point a temporary union of Danielle/Dominique into one person has been accomplished, thus giving us only two celebrants for this murder), she stabs Emil in the groin with the blade. [7] She then staggers away, with Emil wrapped around her, and collapses over Grace's sleeping form. Grace awakens and screams, and De Palma cuts to a shot of an ambulance winding its way up to the clinic where, presumably, the police have the situation in hand.

Although SISTERS ends with Danielle being taken away by the police (as Norman is captured at PSYCHO's finale), neither film leaves us with a proper identification of the real murderer. PSYCHO's psychiatrist claims that "mother killed the girls," yet Mrs. Bates' voice adds a final twist to the proceedings, blaming everything on her son, that "bad" boy. An accurate, exhaustive explanation of the Hitchcock film's events eludes us.

Towards SISTERS' end, Emil plants a hypnotic suggestion in Grace's mind. When asked about the crime, she is to repeat the phrase, "There was no body because there was no murder; it was all a ridiculous mistake." The statement is an obvious inversion of Larch's assertion, when he is following the transported couch, that "you have to have a dead body before you have a murder." Yet both statements lead to dead ends. Although he tells Grace that he finally believes

her story, Detective Kelly can only get Grace to mindlessly
repeat the phrase that Emil has taught her.   Denial takes
precedence over actuality.   Grace denies that there ever was
a murder; therefore, there was no body.

Danielle, being led away from the Institute by the police, states that "I have never hurt anyone in my life," and
maintains that her sister could not have committed the crimes,
since "my sister died last spring."   Both Grace's and Danielle's statements are essentially correct.   Grace's contention
that because there is no corpse no murder has taken place is
accurate in that the first corpse within the film's action is
never found; Philip still reposes in the couch, and even if
Larch does know the couch's location, he is not going to call
the police with this information.   Instead, he intends to wait
around for someone to claim the couch.   And since no one
in Quebec will claim the furniture (both Emil and Danielle
having been effectively eliminated from the picture), the body
will never be discovered.

Danielle's statement reveals a curious mixture of confrontation with and avoidance of the facts.   In one sense, it
is true that she--Danielle--never hurt anyone.   And with her
acceptance of her sister's death (Emil's final legacy to her),
it is suggested that the Dominique personality will never again
emerge.

Strictly speaking, Grace's statement about the first
murder applies to the second as well.   While the police may
have Emil's body, all that they have in the way of suspects
is two women, both blood-spattered and frightened--one (Danielle) denying that a crime has ever been committed, the other
(Grace) unable to testify to a crime's taking place since she
was asleep at the time.   In effect, then, although we have
seen two murders in the film, none really took place.   There
may indeed be two dead bodies somewhere, but the murderer
is inaccessible.   In fact, with Danielle fully accepting her
sister's death, the murderer no longer exists.

As for private detective Larch, and his insistence that
only when the body is claimed will some progress be made
on the case, he is, at SISTERS' end, totally isolated, alone
with both the body and his view of the case's only possible
solution.   Grace cannot act as a witness to any crime; Danielle is now obviously no help.   All that remains is Larch and
his ridiculous insistence that a claimant for the couch will
lead him to the murderer.   What he gets instead--as SIS-

TERS' last shot reveals--is a view of an innocuous covered
couch that stands next to a cow, respective symbols for an
inanimate piece of evidence and the live being joked to it who,
dumb and animal-like, can only chew and re-chew the miserable cud of this convoluted case. Voyeur's binoculars to his
eyes, literally and figuratively up a tree as he dangles from
a telephone pole, Larch is last seen twisting in the wind,
stupidly searching for the explanation that will never come.

As might be expected in a film so strongly concerned with
counterparts and opposite qualities within the same personality, SISTERS contains numerous references to doubles and
doubling. What is surprising about these examples is how
many of them there actually are, especially considering that
this aspect of the film never seems forced, and that within
its 93-minute running time SISTERS manages to establish
numerous characterizations and involve us in some extremely
engaging action at the same time.

I have already mentioned the doubles who appear in
Grace's hallucination sequence, the pairing of the detectives,
and the manner in which Emil attributes two identities to
Grace. The latter example is only one of the numerous
linkages established between Grace and Danielle/Dominique.
After Philip's murder, and immediately following her telephone call to the police, Grace begins to dress in prepara-
tion for her trip over to Danielle's building. At the same
time, via the film's occasional split screen, we see Danielle
dressing. Both women are preparing for their imminent interview with the detectives and each other.

Later, after the film's climactic scenes, we see Grace,
at her parents' home, in the room that (judging by the dolls
and the photos of the Beatles on the walls) she occupied as a
child. Apparently, the shock of the events she has been
through has caused her to regress somewhat, thus placing
her in the position of the helpless child, which is exactly
how the understanding Danielle, the patronizing police, the
smug Larch, the manipulative mother, and the "concerned"
Emil have been treating her all along.

Grace is propped up in bed; to her right is a Raggedy
Ann doll. Together the two figures resemble the paired Dan-
ielle/Dominique (and Grace/Dominique) whom we glimpsed in
SISTERS' earlier scenes. That Grace was seen earlier on
Danielle's right, thus occupying the Dominique position, and

now is seen on the left/Danielle side, with the dead dummy
(Dominique herself is now effectively dead) in the Dominique
position, only further indicates that in the childlike innocence
to which Grace has now retreated (partly out of fear, partly
as a result of Emil's auto-suggestion), she and Danielle are
now one and the same. Danielle sweetly maintains that she
never hurt anyone in her life; Grace joins the innocent sister
in this attitude that proclaims ignorance of evil ("there was
no murder"). That this regression represents a retreat from
SISTERS' apparent advocacy of assertive women and their
rights (this in spite of the film's intentionally stylized brutal
actions) is just a further ironic ending to an already highly
ironic and perplexing film. SISTERS condones female asser-
tiveness as a proper response to male aggression, condemns
murder obliquely, but then shows us its principal female figures retreating to denial. A truly puckish black humor re-
sides behind this attitude, of which Hitchcock would have been
proud.

Dominique's initial "appearance" is preceded by Danielle's search for her sedatives. She finds them, swallows
one, and places the remainder of the bottle's contents on the
sink. Significantly, only two pills remain, just as, after the
murder, the threesome of Danielle/Dominique/Philip will once
again be reduced to the requisite two. The two pills may be
inadvertently knocked down the drain like waste matter, but
it is Philip who is soon to be removed from the apartment
like a disposable piece of garbage that offends the careful
housekeeper with its untidiness. Luckily, Emil stops by to
clean things up.

Almost from SISTERS' outset we are given a dual view
of Emil. At first, in Peeping Toms' audience, he seems an
aberration. The camera tracks past him without lingering,
yet he stands out from the rest of the crowd because of his
cool attire (he is in an overcoat while the rest of the audience is casually dressed); moreover, he is reading a book
instead of paying attention to the admittedly absurd entertainment being provided.

Both at The African Room and outside Danielle's apartment, Emil is seen as a threat, a negative force that prom-
ises to disrupt what appears at first to be a simple romantic
idyll. Philip is smug and suave, a man so cocky and self-
assured that during his drugstore visit for Danielle he buys
himself some shaving cream and a toothbrush, as though he
were planning to move in with the woman for an extended stay.

Later, Philip gloats over his dispatching of Emil, first at the restaurant, then at the apartment ("I got rid of him before and I'll get rid of him again," he says, even though it was the waiters who removed Emil from The African Room, while Philip's ruse to lure Emil away from the apartment fails).

Emil, on the other hand, appears at first to be rash and abrupt, must be dragged out of the restaurant, and is-- unlike the smiling Philip--a disturbing looking figure, with owlish eyes, slicked back hair (Philip's hair is worn natu- rally), and a strikingly red birthmark on his forehead. Later, though, Emil appears in the guise of Danielle's savior, res- cuing her from the awkwardness of the murder scene by his presence of mind and quick actions--activities that contradict our initial impressions of him. He remains throughout the film a dualistic figure, at once sympathetic and alienating, right up to the time of his demise. He is at once a sincere man, trying to make Danielle face the truth about herself and her dead sister, and an evil manipulator/mad-scientist type, who imprisons the helpless Grace against her will and isn't above making advances to a heavily sedated woman (Danielle).

When, during her investigation, Grace stands outside the Linton Clinic and is startled by a shadow on the wall, we can see De Palma actually doubling his own shock devices-- here for both terrifying and comical effects. The two stab wounds inflicted on Philip, which acted as a prelude to the symbolically decisive thrust of the knife into his mouth, are resurrected in the form of a pair of garden shears (two blades) whose shadow (recalling the Dominique-as-shadow who stabs Philip in the mouth) appears on the wall behind Grace and seems to be aiming for her mouth. The fact that the shears are wielded by a Clinic inmate who is clipping an imaginary shrub, and the later revelation that it was with a pair of garden shears that Dominique killed Danielle's baby, make ironic black humor grist out of what was, in its first manifestation, a very real and terrible threat. (One can also read the shadowy attack as a grim retelling of the customary way in which Dominique jealously keeps all out- siders away from her sister. In this case, Grace--who as- sumed the identity of "the other" in the hallucination sequence --is properly threatened, albeit in a mock fashion.)

In this scene, we are not only given an allusive warn- ing about what might happen to Grace if she pursues her in- vestigation (will she meet the same fate as Philip?), but an example of the type of humor that pervades SISTERS. Nu-

merous scenes and shots come to mind: the scene in which
Emil, after the murder, trips on the floor while trying to
cart away the bloody linen (clearly a repetition of Grace's
dropping of another piece of evidence: the Danielle/Domi-
nique birthday cake); the scene in which Grace's mother,
after her daughter's interrogation of the bakery workers,
steps in with the impromptu excuse that Grace's abruptness
is due to newspaper deadlines; or Mrs. Collier's later inquiry about whether Grace's fanatical devotion to her story
is due to her "taking those diet pills again."

Even private detective Larch gets into the black comedy act, telling Grace that she may know reporting (although
he mistakenly refers to her job as "magazine work") but he
knows detection. "I went to the Brooklyn Institute of Modern
Investigation, " he says with a straight face.

Perhaps most striking among SISTERS' instances of
doubling is its use of the split screen. This device, employed in CARRIE and BLOW OUT as well, is here used to
give the audience two simultaneous views of concurrent action, thus avoiding the fragmentation occasioned by montage
editing while communicating twice the normal amount of picture information within the same frame. Employed when
Philip drags himself to the window while Grace stares into
Danielle's apartment, when Emil runs down the hallway while
Grace and the detectives are coming up the elevator, and
when Danielle is being questioned by Kelly and Grace at her
door, the split screen has a dual effect on us. It is at once
unifying and divisive, in that we simultaneously are given a
more comprehensive vision of events but only through a necessary eye-scan back and forth between the two images. The
tension between these two tendencies--between the urge to
fragmentation and the urge towards unity--can be seen not
only as a thematic device complementing the film's tense action, but also as a subtle reflection of SISTERS' dominant
character: Danielle/Dominique, who at each moment of the
film veers between unification (bought at the price of sedation
and denial) and fragmentation, a jumping back and forth between her live and dead identities. It is precisely Danielle's
inability to live successfully in either of these worlds (even
at SISTERS' end, she is still deluding herself by denying the
murders) that makes her, in spite of her reprehensible actions, such a sympathetic figure.

Like PSYCHO's evocation of varying psychological states
through the use of tones of black and white (the darkness of

the Bates home as a reflection of repressed fears and desires; the movement from the glare of Phoenix to the stormy
uncertainties of the highway during Marion's flight), SISTERS
employs subtle color schemes to complement its polarities.
As the blind girl, Danielle combines innocence (her feigned
inability to see what is going on around her) and experience
(her apparent sexual maturity) in the white of her blouse and
the blackness of her jacket. Similarly, she evokes the innocence of Danielle and the evil of Dominique in the white
negligee she dons for Philip and the black sweater that, as
Dominique, she wears during the murder--a sweater that disappears (apparently removed in the bathroom, where the twins
were first revealed) after the crime is committed. When the
detectives come to question her, she reverts to the necessary
color scheme connoting innocence (perhaps at least partially
as a result of Emil's insisting that she cloak her guilt by
"Put[ting] on some make-up") as the white nightgown again
appears.

        Emil complements Danielle in these color changes.
He cloaks his identity in the studio and in the street by wear-
ing a black overcoat; yet when he begins to clean up the dis-
array in the murder's wake, he reverts to a white topcoat,
virtually willing the apartment into cleanliness. Looking
somewhat surgeon-like (his outer garment resembles a lab
coat), he removes all (well, almost all) traces of body and
blood from the premises. [8]

        The immediate vicinity of the murder scene itself
evokes a powerful contrariety of impulses. The redness of
the building's hallways suggests both passion and the inner
(vaginal?) recesses of the body, while the whiteness of Danielle's apartment hints at the innocent room of Danielle's personality to which she retreats after the crime--a room spat-
tered with Philip's blood but restored to whiteness (at least
temporarily) by Emil.

        Unfortunately, the prime piece of furniture in the
apartment--the couch on which Danielle and Philip make love,
and from which Danielle/Dominique kills Philip--is the one
piece of whiteness in the apartment whose blood traces are
neither noticed nor removed. Danielle, Emil, the detectives,
Grace, Larch, the moving men--no one notices the blood stain
on the couch's back, the red blotch of which (like the rose-
colored spot that stands out against Emil's white forehead)
functions indelibly as a fine contradictory symbol of the opposing impulses towards innocence and mayhem inherent not

only in Danielle/Dominique's personality but within the film
as well.

SISTERS is a wry and well-tuned piece of cinematic
frenzy. With the exception of the inexcusable (albeit dramatically necessary) trick of showing us a fantasy sequence
as though it were really taking place (the Danielle/talking-
shadow Dominique conversation), it is an irreproachable film,
sufficiently unified and dramatically impressive enough to establish De Palma as a filmmaker of the first order.

NOTES

1. One can also view this recurrent ambiguity as a form of
    doubling that in meaning nicely complements the physi-
    cal doubling of the film's characters.
2. We must assume that Danielle's delayed personality change
    at this point is due more to dramatic necessity than
    character consistency, since her later change into
    Dominique occurs quite rapidly.
3. Sample column titles include "Staten Islanders--Who Are
    We?," "The Lost Borough," and "Why We Call Them
    Pigs."
4. The title of SISTERS alone suggests that in one respect
    the film is about feminism and proposes the necessity
    of recognizing the oppression of women. In fact, this
    is precisely the approach taken by Robin Wood (cf. the
    Bibliography and the interview with De Palma).
        Yet in an important sense, to read the film this
    way is to fail to deal with it on its own terms. While
    the relationship between power and sexuality is ad-
    dressed in SISTERS, to transform the film into a
    feminist tract is not only to do the film a critical in-
    justice, but also to dangerously ignore the manner in
    which--as a film primarily "constructed" to create
    suspense--it is meant to thrill as well as edify. Ad-
    ditionally, it should be noted that while the men in
    SISTERS are repaid for their manipulations, the man-
    ner in which they are upbraided (murder) can only be
    approved on a fictive, not a "real," basis.
5. Mrs. Collier's blatant concern with the way that her
    daughter is leading her life smacks of voyeurism as
    well, of a relentless probing into other people's af-
    fairs. This view of her no doubt explains why--in
    the later hallucination sequence--Mrs. Collier appears
    as a gawking onlooker who thrusts herself up near
    Danielle and Dominique and snaps their picture.

6. Ironically, it is as a result of this operation--which
    causes Dominique's death--that the murdering sister
    actually begins to have a true life of her own. Act-
    ing through the pliable Danielle, the Dominique per-
    sonality finally begins totally to have its way any time
    it wants to, coming and going at will, unencumbered
    by a physical yoking to its twin. Moreover, all of
    Dominique's murders can be read as re-enactments
    of her own knife-murder at Emil's hands. Previously,
    Dominique had attempted (successfully, it seems) to
    kill Danielle's baby who--like the men close to Dani-
    elle who are seen in the film--threatened to come be-
    tween the two sisters. The baby, the third member,
    is--like Philip and Emil--eliminated, and the sisterly
    duo are (until the film's unusual ending) once again a
    solitary two.
7. The doctor who, in Dominique's view, killed her with a
    scalpel is appropriately dispatched with the same kind
    of implement.
8. A lapse in continuity during this scene results in Emil's
    wearing a beige-colored coat during one brief shot.

It takes an audacious and fun-loving director to yoke together
THE PHANTOM OF THE OPERA with Faust, grand opera
with rock music, adding to the mixture elements from PSY-
CHO, The Picture of Dorian Gray, and ROCK AROUND THE
CLOCK--yet De Palma is clearly equal to the task.   THE
PHANTOM OF THE PARADISE, De Palma's intentionally
hokey pastiche of percussion and perversion, has all of the
graveyard humor of some of the more renowned depression-
era cartoons, works like Ub Iwerks' SPOOKS and THE
CUCKOO MURDER CASE and an old, virtually forgotten Paul
Terry cartoon whose main character is haunted by the spir-
its of Bach, Beethoven, and Brahms, who rise from their
graves crying "you stole my symphony" when the composers'
tunes have been shamelessly "borrowed."

In the manner in which it crazily veers between dialogue and action that seem intentionally satirical and relevant, as opposed to characterizations and techniques so blatantly stylized that they appear to revel in their artificiality,
PHANTOM resembles what it implicitly criticizes: the music industry that steals, metamorphoses, and packages ster-
eotypical attitudes about love, sex, and death and sells them
to a generation of consumers in such an insidious way that
the audience believes that their innermost dreams and desires are given voice.

Rock music is an indigenous American phenomenon,
eminently characteristic of the country from which it springs

30

in that it is both populist and elitist at the same time. The
"secret knowledge" about rebelliousness and teenage love, the
despising of conventionality, of parents and their "straight,"
conformist universe is, in the music world, expressed by
"loners"--Dylan, Elvis--who reach their "selective" audience
through million-dollar banks of sound recorders, record
presses, and multi-nationally owned distribution networks
that revamp and package this "non-conformist" product like
so much washpowder. The men who market the teen dreams
are members of the class that these rebels condemn in their
music, dress, and life styles.

The act of creating a film engages the writer, director, and actors in a similarly consumer-conscious, multi-
leveled series of deals. For PHANTOM--a serio-comic
critique of the rock music milieu--to have taken itself seriously would thus have been a grievous mistake. That it does
not, and still manages to retain the sense of enjoyment and
feel for experimentation that characterized De Palma's earlier
films, demonstrates that with this, his third "commercial"
film, De Palma has already become knowledgeable about the
demands of the marketplace. PHANTOM is not, then, just
a film about the youth market; it is a product for that market as well, with the difference that it is--and this is its
saving grace--an extremely well-wrought, self-conscious
product.

As the film's opening song reveals, PHANTOM is the
story of "the ultimate rock palace, the man who made it, the
girl who sang in it, the man who stole it."[1] We meet Swan
(Paul Williams), the head of Death Records (their corporate
symbol: a dead black bird) who made (or more precisely is
going to make) the Paradise Theatre the place for rock entertainment; Winslow (William Finley), the composer whose music is stolen by Swan; and Phoenix (Jessica Harper)--the young
woman they are both involved with, who sings Winslow's rock
opera about Faust, first the way he wants her to sing it (when
he prompts her in the waiting line at Swan's house), later the
way that Swan wants it done, at The Paradise, where she is
appearing as a back-up singer for the appropriately named
Beef (Gerrit Graham).

In his first few appearances, Swan is never glimpsed
whole. After the Juicy Fruits (later to become the Beach
Bums, then The Undead, thus proving that having many iden-
tities--which is tantamount to having none--is the only way to
endure in the music world) finish the opening title song, Swan

gives their performance cool approval by clapping his white-
gloved hands together slowly, quietly; all we see are his
hands.   Later, we are exposed to his voice, then to his reflection in a mirror.   It is only after PHANTOM has pro-
gressed significantly into the first reel that the much-
anticipated Swan makes his grand entrance, finally emerging as a character having both physical and aural presence.
By that point, we already know about his leadership of the
music industry, how he doesn't hire stars, he creates them.
To further reinforce the associations already developed about
Swan and his role in the film, De Palma assigns the part to
songwriter/performer Paul Williams.   Physically, Williams
lends a puckish deviltry to Swan's character.   The contrast
between the power his character wields and Williams' slight-
ness of build sets up an annoying tension.   Nor is Williams
an overly attractive man.   His baby blonde hair and pudgy,
virtually infantile features suggest a well-fed homunculus or
an other-worldly changeling left on someone's doorstep.[2]
Swan is a fully-grown character desiring wealth, power,
fame, but in the body of a child, compensating for this con-
tradiction by brutally manipulating those around him: from
his stooge, Philbin, to the aspiring group of singers who
must physically "perform" for him (first among themselves,
only later with Swan) to gain a possible break for what they
imagine to be their careers.

We know virtually from the beginning of the film that
Swan not only sells death, he is death; he represents mortality and destruction for both Winslow and Phoenix (although
the latter character rises out of Winslow and Swan's ashes
at the end of the film).   The combined fear of and attraction
to death is powerfully represented through Swan, who profits
by and packages mortality, but who in reality provides only
the semblance of death, a dalliance with the morbid through
singers like The Undead, whose make-up is a direct steal
from the destructively-pitched rock group Kiss.

Apparently, this vicarious death is what the audience
wants, and Mr. Death himself is there to give it to them.
Rock music has always had a pronounced streak of morbidity
in it, not only in song ("Teen Angel" is the most outstanding
example) but in the legends that grew up around rock stars
who either died accidentally (Buddy Holly, Richie Valens,
The Big Bopper, Otis Redding, Jim Croce) or as a result
of their own self-destructiveness (Janis Joplin, Elvis Pres-
ley, Jim Morrison, Jimi Hendrix).   This cult-like worshiping
of rock's dead idols--with destruction a necessary prelude to

apotheosis--suggests that one of rock music's strongest undercurrents is a pronounced need for the mythic, for a <u>Golden
Bough</u>-like death of the god as a necessary prelude to re-
juvenation of the land and resurrection of the deity.   That
PHANTOM's plot inevitably moves towards just such a de-
nouement--with the new star Phoenix born again when Beef,
Swan, and Winslow are dead--indicates how successfully the
film has captured and portrayed this structure.

        The packaging of death naturally has powerful com-
mercial possibilities.   Thus Death Records, their music and
performers, all cater directly to destruction and evisceration
as evidenced in the Frankenstein-like opera of The Dead at
the film's end; the cutting up of the fans by the knife-like
edges of the group's guitars; the awesomeness of the power
of the audience (which acts as a single entity) going after the
performers to tear off a piece of their clothing or, perhaps
preferably, their flesh.   Death Records and its head, Swan,
appropriate these powerful mythic undercurrents, with one
important difference: while accomplished in death (both
through representations of it in performance and through the
many performers like Winslow whom Swan has, no doubt
successfully, buried alive) the company cannot achieve re-
births.   Mock resurrections may be performed on stage, but
the only real revitalization that occurs in PHANTOM belongs
to Phoenix once she has repudiated Swan and his philosophy
(which is, appropriately, totally death-oriented, without the
faintest signs of life).

        PHANTOM beautifully captures the crowd psychology
of rock in its songs and production numbers.   The jumping,
screaming audience at The Paradise becomes the tool of the
artists on stage.   When Beef, in the guise of the dead Frankenstein come to life, sings his evisceration song, the audience accordingly responds with yells and screams.   Yet the
crowd--gone wild with the blood lust of the music's pulsing
bass beat and the crescendo of Beef's cannibalistic cries--is
soon satisfied, and they can immediately settle back in their
seats and listen in absolute silence when Phoenix sings her
tender ballad.   That the performance of her song is only
made possible by Beef's death is obvious to everyone concerned: to Swan, who allows it; to Phoenix, who takes advantage of it; and to Winslow, who kills Beef so that Phoenix
might rise from his ashes, which smolder on stage throughout her performance.   The suggestion underlying the scene
brings us back to another practice covered in <u>The Golden
Bough</u>; here animal (Beef) sacrifice seems necessary in order that calm, for a time at least, might prevail.

Yet such placidity--in the film and in the rock world
that it portrays in microcosm--is short-lived. No sooner
does Phoenix finish her song than she sells herself to Swan
in exchange for the noise of applause, which apparently cap-
tivates her far more than Winslow's music and its lyrics
calling for trust and forgiveness.

This is not to suggest that PHANTOM proposes a simple opposition in rock music between the forces of life and
death, since neither Winslow nor Swan represents life or
death by himself. Thus Winslow, the humble, dedicated
composer who has authored a whole rock opera about the
Faust legend, only appears to be a simple individual. As
a performer, he is not only second-rate (as Swan correctly
points out while listening to him; what matters is his music)
but is also strongly involved in an intense form of narcissism. This view of Winslow is suggested by the manner in
which his soulfully-sung ballad near the film's opening is delivered (a ballad sung with all of the gestures of forced candor and feigned humility recognizable to anyone who has ever
watched a performer "sell" a song with inflections, body
movements, and wet looks at the camera while the head is
tilted at just the right thoughtful angle), as well as by the
camera movement that De Palma elects to use at this point.
The 360-degree pan draws a narcissistic circle around Winslow, who in this sequence is clearly only interested in himself.

As for Swan, he is not only death. Representing overt
consumerism (exemplified by his house, its lush interiors,
and the manner in which he so successfully peddles the prod-
ucts of Death Records), he becomes an emblem of the world.
He is already the Devil (although this aspect will be somewhat modified at PHANTOM's end), the Mephistopheles to
whom Winslow/Faust sells his soul, his music. Completing
the tripartite equation, Swan is the flesh as well, an aspect
suggested by his maintenance of a harem of singers and the
manner in which his dress pampers the adipose, infantile
flesh (which we later learn has been permanently purchased
at a high cost) that he drags around with him.

Yet there is a strong suggestion that the relationship
between Winslow and Swan is more than that of Devil and
slave, Mephistopheles and Faust. True, Winslow gains notoriety and knowledge (in this case, of good and evil, love
and death) through his association with Swan. Yet neither
character is represented as having anything approaching a

sexual identity, which suggests a strong affinity between them.
Phoenix, on the other hand, is clearly female. Her dancing
while performing evidences a successful use of her body,
while she refuses to allow herself to be seduced by Philbin
in Swan's house (and, as she points out, it is never clear
whether she is auditioning for the role of singer or concu-
bine).

Winslow, although he protests Swan's theft of his man-
uscript and invades his fortress trying to recover it, almost
immediately begins to relinquish the small amount of sexual
identity he has. Trying to get in to see Swan by any means
available to him Winslow, dressed in what appears to be a
dowdy housewife's shift, secretes himself among Swan's con-
cubines. When he is thrown out, with Swan significantly
commenting, "Get that faggot out of here," he is accosted
by two policemen, who swiftly draw the conclusion that he
is some sort of male prostitute. In prison, he is compelled
to have all of his teeth extracted, the loss suggesting a de-
cline in sexual potency too blatant to be overlooked.

Like the phantom portrayed in the 1925, 1943 and 1962
film versions of the story, Winslow's courtship of his female
singer-love is indirect, mostly confined to his adulation of
her while she performs. It is the woman in PHANTOM OF
THE PARADISE who takes the active role in this curious relationship. Winslow is closest to Phoenix only when she is
singing his music, which suggests that what really excites
and satisfies him is not the singer but the song. And since
the song is his, we can only conclude that his narcissism
still reigns; as in the ballad he performs towards PHAN-
TOM's beginning, he is making love to himself through his
music.

Swan's sexuality is also suspect. It is difficult to
imagine what kind of sexual self-image this short, baby-
faced entrepreneur can have; he looks quite uncomfortable
in his body. The insular aspect of self-love evident in Winslow is manifest in Swan as well. Thus, the members of
Swan's harem significantly comment that he would probably
rather watch them having sex with each other than enter into
the frolicking as a participant. And when Swan is finally
given a love scene, he takes (like Winslow) a recessive role;
Phoenix makes all of the advances. She opens his shirt,
kisses his chest, runs her fingers through his fine hair.
Only when Swan realizes that Winslow the phantom is watching this whole scene through the skylight does he begin to

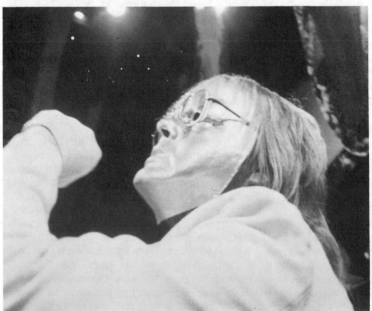

take apparent pleasure in the situation (and who can tell if
his actions at this point are real or merely contrived to make
Winslow--who is apparently Swan's true love--jealous?), although he scarcely moves from his laid-back position.

The suggestion here is obvious: the real sexual couple
(in fact, the only sexual couple) in PHANTOM is Winslow and
Swan, the two lovers--one a writer, one a producer, the man
who creates the product and the man who packages it--who
are so enamored of themselves (thus Winslow's narcissism and
Swan's narcissistically-motivated Dorian Gray pact) that each
can only give expression to his love through contact, however
vicarious, with the only other character who is so totally like
him in a death-oriented preference of fame and power over
love and devotion. Both having sold out, their only pleasures
lie in gazing upon their own corruptions as reflected in each
other. [3] In Winslow, Swan sees the creator that he will never
be; while in Swan, Winslow envisions the man who makes
things happen, the source of money and influence without
whom his music will never reach the world. The two attract like fatal polarities: Swan the doer, the Apollonian,
Winslow the creator, the Dionysian. They meet in a music-
filled rock palace of light and sound in order to reach con-
summation through their singer/proxy, the woman who asserts
and sings at the same time: Phoenix.

The ultimate clash of these two complementary characters occurs on the night of Swan's proposed marriage to Phoenix, an event that will take place live on stage at The Paradise. Yet the ceremony is never completed, as though no
true sexual union could ever occur in PHANTOM's universe. [4]

Only the wedding could possibly serve as the true merger
of the instincts of destruction (Swan) and regeneration (Phoenix). Swan, knowing that such a marriage could never take
place without a complete alteration of his values and priori-
ties (even in corrupted form, Phoenix still has the taint of
vitality about her), arranges for Phoenix to be assassinated
on stage; death is the instrument that will bring them together.
The marksman misses, however, killing the Bishop (Philbin)
instead. By this point, Winslow has already discovered how
unreal and insidiously evil Swan's actual existence really is.

[Opposite:] PHANTOM's two real lovers: at top, Winslow
(William Finley) and, below, Swan (Paul Williams). Note
the similar physical attitudes and mask materials.

Rummaging through Swan's videotape collection, Winslow discovers that Swan is not, as he had believed, the ultimate,
true plenipotentiary of evil, but only a minor devil, one of
the lesser malefactors. On the brink of middle age, Swan
made a pact with a devil more powerful than the one he is
to become (who could only grant fame and fortune to mortals).
Swan contracted for eternal youth, a truly Faustian bargain
whose enormity Winslow no doubt secretly admires.

The Dorian Gray screw is given a final turn by De
Palma, though, for in Swan's case, if his young-looking videotape image is destroyed, he will revert to his true age (a bit
silly, since how long ago can Swan have made the pact, rock
music being only 24 years old at the time of PHANTOM's
production). Armed with the tape, Winslow watches from
The Paradise's wings as Philbin dies. Having already dispatched Beef with an appropriately modern neon thunderbolt,
Winslow swings down from the rafters before the ceremony's
end and destroys the tape, whereupon both Swan and Winslow
are truly unmasked. Swan immediately grows old; Winslow
stabs Swan, the wound causing (as Swan said such a wound
might) a sympathetic wound on Winslow's body, thus affirming their symbiotic relationship as doppelganger counterparts.

All that remains at PHANTOM's end is Phoenix, now
twice-risen from the ashes, first from the smoldering flames
of Beef's demise, now released thanks to the conflagrant meeting of Winslow and Swan in death. Winslow's slow victory is
accomplished; he has, albeit indirectly, given his Phoenix-
love new life, while Swan's song is finished. Whether all of
this action suggests a rebirth for rock music as well is impossible to determine with any assurance. Yet if one remem-
bers that with all of the talk about the great Paradise, the
theatre is barely glimpsed at all in the film (it seems to exist more as meeting place than actual haven); the implicit suggestion is that while a release from destruction is possible,
there is no Paradise (either real rock palace or mythical
Eden) to return to. Whether it be through Miltonic "diso-
bedience" or the corrupting influences of commercially-
oriented pop music, Paradise is forever forfeit. There is
no way back to harmony and oneness. As Swan comments
at one point, "Nothing matters anyway; that's the hell of it."
Creation in the face of meaningless--endeavors like those of
Winslow, Swan, and De Palma as well--seem to be the only
worthwhile actions left.

De Palma is thus very much like a combination Wins-

low/Swan, composing the verses of his film, then packaging
and marketing them for profit.   All three "characters" diddle
in the midst of a godless universe within which redemption
(if it is at all possible) is gained only through our own la-
bors, and within which we can, apparently, do little except
keep ourselves busy to drown out the awful silence.   De Palma
is capable of successfully proclaiming this situation, and proclaiming it well.   PHANTOM, in its playful way, catches
traces of the divine; SISTERS and (as we shall see) CARRIE
capture it whole.

NOTES

1.   See also the chapter on CARRIE for the notable ways in
     which De Palma uses music to communicate or com-
     plement a sequence's themes.
2.   De Palma will continue to exploit the distasteful aspects
     of various actors in future productions.   Thus, John
     Travolta in CARRIE, Cliff Robertson in OBSESSION,
     John Cassavetes in THE FURY, Angie Dickinson in
     DRESSED TO KILL, and John Lithgow (in both OB-
     SESSION and BLOW OUT) successfully play charac-
     ters whose unattractiveness is due in no small part
     to the way the actors look in these films.   (A glance
     back at the still of William Finley from SISTERS
     should quickly indicate how well this adaptable actor
     --who looks so different in PHANTOM--made his ap-
     pearance suitably alienating to reflect the ambiguous
     role he plays in the earlier film.   Astute viewers
     will recognize Finley as the unkempt psychic, Ray-
     mond, who is briefly seen tailing Gillian in THE
     FURY.)
3.   The theme of the voyeur--which was so intelligently in-
     vestigated in SISTERS--is obviously present here.
     Winslow watches Swan and Phoenix through the sky-
     light and observes Phoenix from the wings of The
     Paradise.   Swan, with his closed-circuit television
     receivers and his bathroom mirror narcissistic pact
     with the devil, is also a watcher, though possibly of
     a more insidious kind.
4.   The culmination of the love-night liaison between Swan
     and Phoenix is never graphically represented; its ab-
     sence from the screen severely limits its reality for
     the audience.

The most striking characteristic of OBSESSION is its unified tone. Much of this unity stems from Paul Schrader's script which was--at composer Bernard Herrmann's suggestion-- trimmed so that the film ended in 1975 instead of 1980. [1] But most, if not all, of OBSESSION's economy (on second and third viewings the film moves very quickly and effort- lessly) derives from the singularity of its story and its main character, Michael Courtland (Cliff Robertson), whose fixa- tion on the memories of his dead wife and daughter prevents De Palma from doing much else except delineating Michael's psychology and the manner in which he deals with the "mi- raculous" reappearance of his dead wife, Elizabeth, in the person of Sandra Portinari (both played by Genevieve Bujold), whom he meets sixteen years after his wife's death in the same church where he and Elizabeth first became acquainted. [2]

Referring to the opening scene in PSYCHO between Sam Loomis and Marion Crane, Raymond Durgnat, in Focus on Hitchcock, remarked that the characters' entire conversa- tion centered on sex and money. [3] The same holds true for the relationship between Michael and Elizabeth in OBSESSION's early sequences. Although Michael's partner, Robert La Salle (John Lithgow), remarks during the opening scene's anniver- sary party that Michael and Elizabeth represent the last ro- mantics in his generation, this assertion is quickly undercut. In toasting the couple, La Salle refers to Michael as "a man of endless energy and ambition." The latter quality is the important one here. OBSESSION gives us testimonials in dia-

logue form from Robert indicating that Michael is really not
that interested in amassing large amounts of money (e.g.,
the statements about Michael's insistence that the Pontchartrain property have plenty of trees [presumably instead of
condominiums]; and his complaints about how much money
the two of them could have made if Michael had been more
acquisitive), but the main action of the film gives the lie to
these claims. Instead, we see Michael on the eve of his
wedding anniversary waiting for his wife to undress and fon-
dling a black felt box (presumably containing a present of expensive jewelry for Elizabeth)--a box which, significantly, he
is still tightly holding onto throughout the couple's entire embrace.

After Elizabeth and daughter Amy are kidnapped, and
Michael is persuaded by Inspector Brie (a cheesy detective?)
to pay off the kidnappers with blank paper instead of money,
the kidnappers flee with their captives. Later everyone--kid-
nappers, Amy, and Elizabeth--seems to die in a fiery colli-
sion with a gasoline truck. The viewer has already noted
that the money Michael was going to have used to pay the
ransom would originally have been employed to purchase his
part of the option on the Pontchartrain property. Since the
kidnappers are not paid with real money, Michael uses this
cash to pick up his share of the option and--after the tragic
crash--to build on the undeveloped land a monolithic structure
which (we soon realize) is a small-scale version of the church
within which he and Elizabeth first met.

The significance of this monument cannot be overlooked.
Although Michael would doubtless assert that the structure is
a testimonial to his love for his wife and daughter, an expression of his grief over their deaths, the monument seems
more like an ostentatious flaunting of grief, a large stone
carving placed in the middle of "some of the richest land in
the South," as Robert refers to it, as though some great and
obviously expensive creation were necessary to prove just how
selfless Michael's love for his dead wife and daughter really
is.

On the contrary, the monument seems excessive, and
can easily lead one to conclude that its owner is for some
reason compensating for his lack of internal grief and despair
by making a large, public, graphic display of his sorrow.
Jesus' critical remarks on penance and public works are ap-
posite here: "... when ye fast, be not, as the hypocrites,
of a sad countenance: for they disfigure their faces, that they

The South's "perfect couple": Michael (Cliff Robertson), cold as usual, and his wealthily-bedecked wife, Elizabeth (Genevieve Bujold).

may appear unto men to fast ... but thou, when thou fastest, anoint thine head, and wash thy face; That thou appear not unto men to fast, but unto thy Father which is in secret" (Matthew 6:16-18). "All their [the Scribes' and Pharisees'] works they do for to be seen of men: they make broad their phylacteries, and enlarge the borders of their garments ... " (Matthew 23:5).

Viewing Michael's actions in light of the above statements makes the kidnapper's comments to Amy about the counterfeit cash ("this is what your old man thinks you're worth--nothing") ironically relevant. On both occasions in the film when Michael tries to ransom his loved one(s), the payoff is in phony money. And while it is true that the first substitution was with Michael's knowledge while the second was not, it is also true that at neither time is he able successfully to redeem his wife or daughter (potential wife/real daughter in the second instance) with money. It is no more possible for Michael to buy back his future "wife" in 1975 than it was for him to ransom his wife and daughter in 1959. In both cases, his reliance upon money rather than emotional devotion as a tool of reclamation dooms the redemptions (and, without a change in him, the relationships) to failure.

It is money that Michael sees as a bond between people, not love. In this sense, Robert--who throughout the film represents the acquisitive side of Michael's personality, but in a coarse incarnation (thus his tactless repetition to the Italians of Michael's remark about their "wives")--unknowingly carries out (through his blackmail plot) the spirit of Michael's obsession about money and love somehow being related, with the former fixation eventually dominating and supplanting the latter. The precise wording of Michael's remark about the Italians is thus highly ironic given this yoking of love and money, since when Michael asks, "How come these rich men all seem to have young wives?" he is unconsciously criticizing the confluence of passion and finance of which he himself is already guilty, and at the same time anticipating the substance of his future relationship with Sandra.

That money, not emotional spirit, is all that Michael has to offer Sandra Portinari (who is really his grown-up daughter, Amy)[4] is quite clear. While Sandra has her work on the crumbling picture of the Madonna, all that Michael has is his business. "What do you do?" she asks, and he replies, "I'm in land development." The statement is followed by an awkward pause. The distinction between working with art to

create (or in this case restore, a creative act in itself) and
working with money merely to make more money is painfully
obvious.   Michael is a hollow man, was so before his wife
and daughter were abducted (thus the entry in Elizabeth's diary, "Sometimes I wonder if Mike loves me as much as his
business"), and remains so now. [5]   That Sandra/Amy is privy
to part of Robert's plot to relieve Michael of both the Pontchartrain property and half a million dollars only makes it
clearer that the relationship between her and Michael (like
the one between Michael and her mother) is at this point
based on wealth alone, thus linking her in attitude with her
father.

     If any further proof of this view were necessary, one
need only recall the hospital scene in which the woman posing
as mother Portinari is dying.   The old woman asks Michael
only two questions, both pertinent and related to each other:
"Are you rich?" and "Do you love my Sandra?"   The suggestion is that only the dead or near-dead yoke love and money
together in such a blatant fashion.   Significantly, De Palma
at this point has Robertson smile in a chillingly insidious
way.   This gesture, combined with the scene's lighting--
which makes Robertson's eyes look small and squinted, virtually porcine--tells us a great deal about the relationship
between love and money in the film.   Michael's money does
not bring him life, but is instead used to build monuments
to the dead (presumably, he helps Sandra purchase an appropriate burial place for her mother).   How intimately Michael's
wealth is involved with death can be seen in his acquisition of
monuments to his emotional involvements; these monuments,
however, instead of memorializing the dead, testify rather to
Michael's emotional living death.   Like Sandra, who also acts
emotionlessly (feigning romantic involvement with Michael in
order to swindle him out of money and pay him back for not
ransoming her and Elizabeth), Michael channels all his emotional
energy into a death-oriented obsession with wealth.   Regardless
of whether he disdains it, and no matter how many lucrative
deals he passes up, Michael only shows animation (and then
only a little) when using his money to buy back love, either
by attempting to ransom it when it is captured or, in the
present instance, by purchasing a new wife to replace the old.

     Viewed in this way, many of OBSESSION's speeches
take on new meaning.   The question posed to Michael by Sandra about the painting of the madonna she is working on
(should we "restore the original," which would mean that we
would "never know for sure what lies beneath it" or delve be-

Death as the only common bond.   Michael and Sandra/Amy
in OBSESSION.

low to possibly uncover a hidden artistic treasure?) gives
rise to Michael's telling answer: "Hold onto it; beauty should
be protected, " he says.   This is precisely what Michael himself is doing: holding onto the vision of his original wife,
whom he means to restore to life by marrying her double.
Not once does he attempt to question his underlying motives,
or to wonder about the oddity of Sandra's resemblance to
Elizabeth.

That Michael's fixation is morbid is suggested by his
psychiatrist, Dr. Ellman, who only refers to the matter obliquely.   No one in OBSESSION ever gives voice explicitly to
Michael's problem.   Instead, the film's meanings are intentionally restricted to those suggested in action or dialogue,
with the consequence that virtually every scene takes on ironic
significance due to the two ways in which it can be read: one
superficial and objective, one probing and psychologically-
oriented.   Michael's answer to Sandra affirms his belief that

he will, by restoring the original (Elizabeth) to him, at the same time somehow rejuvenate his emotional life as well.

The obsession with the dead come back to life recalls Poe's "Ligeia." In that story, the narrator believes that the spirit of his first wife has returned to inhabit the body of his second wife, who has died mysteriously. The elements of money-fixation and death-fixation that occur in OBSESSION occur in "Ligeia" as well.[6] The narrator is a rich man, rich enough to be idle and non-productive, and free thereby to give full reign to his morbid fascinations. "I had no lack of what the world calls wealth."

Like Michael, "Ligeia's" narrator surrounds himself with reminders of death. His sleeping chamber is, for example, decorated with "sarcophagi" and other morbid furnishings. Also like Michael, the narrator only seems to realize the full significance of his love for his wife through her death. "In death only was I fully impressed with the strength of her affection" (the ambiguous syntax suggests that both Ligeia and the narrator are "in death," apparently the one mortally, the other emotionally). Finally, substituting for OBSESSION's contemporary stress on psychological aberration as the root of action is "Ligeia's" narrator's addiction to opium, which nevertheless fails to qualify as an exhaustive explanation for the narrator's psychology.

OBSESSION's story about a dead first wife whose double miraculously returns (thus the madonna-like backlighting of Sandra when, resembling an apparition, she first appears, as well as the swelling choir music that accompanies this shot), is a subtle reworking of Poe's theme, with the twist that where in "Ligeia" the two women at first seem entirely opposite in physical characteristics, in OBSESSION, Elizabeth and Sandra/Amy appear as doubles.

When Sandra, quoting from Dante (himself fixated on a younger woman), tells Michael, "in life do not be inconstant to your lady who in death doth lie," she is giving voice to the morbid philosophy that "Ligeia's" narrator lived by, and the implied consequence that a fixation on death leaves no room for the living (the narrator's lack of attentiveness to his second wife doubtless contributed to her death). Michael, then, should not be pursuing his relationship with Sandra--a curious statement for the girl to make since without the successful completion of the courtship there would be no revenge.

Yet Sandra's quote has another meaning that eludes both her and Michael until OBSESSION's end. The word "lie" may refer both to a prone position and to prevarication. Again, Sandra is implicitly warning Michael to ignore the urgings of the dead, the emotionless in him. Death's verity is that devotion to life is the highest truth, an attitude that would consequently brand both Michael and Amy/Sandra as traitors to life. One can, ultimately, only be constant to one's dead lady by living as fully and meaningfully as possible, thus vitalizing her memory with one's own actions.

Michael's inability to grieve openly about his dead wife and daughter is communicated in a remark he makes to Sandra after telling her that he was stationed in Italy at the end of the second World War. "I'm not really an expert on occupation; my mind is elsewhere," he says, giving voice to his estrangement from his own curative impulses in a statement whose applicability he fails to realize.

De Palma uses a 360-degree pan (a device employed with great success in CARRIE) at three key points in OBSESSION. The technique first appears in a clockwise pan around the Pontchartrain property which bridges the gap between 1959 and the "present time" of the film. At the pan's end it is 1975, Michael (seen at the shot's beginning) is older looking, and the monument is in place. The second pan is also used to convey the passage of time, but in a more subtle way. Sandra is in the master bedroom, looking through some of Elizabeth's things. The pan, similarly clockwise, begins with her rummaging through a drawer, and ends with her reading the previously quoted entry from Elizabeth's diary. The entry is communicated by an off-camera reading which, in giving voice to Elizabeth's voiceless words, seems to move her into the present for us, as though she were still alive (which, in one sense, she is, in the person of her daughter, who for a time is assuming her role).

Throughout OBSESSION, the viewer has been pulled in two different directions: forward in time as the story progresses, backward in time with the evocations of Michael's obsession with the past. The stage has now been set for a resolution of these contrary impulses, which will occur after some significant intervening action.

In OBSESSION's last scenes, Michael and Sandra are freed from their fixations. Sandra realizes how vile and manipulative "Uncle" Robert really is and how, underneath, Michael is a good man and grieving parent. She attempts to cut her wrists with a manicuring scissors while on a plane back to Italy. Michael similarly benefits from a skirmish with death which relieves him of his death-oriented obsession. Also using a pair of scissors, he frees himself by stabbing his reprehensibly acquisitive alter ego, Robert ("Do you realize how rich we could have been?" Robert asks shortly before his murder). Bloodletting in both instances breaks the deadly cycle, thus permitting the family reunion that is soon to take place.

At the airport, Michael and Sandra--each aware of the other's true identity (Michael as loving father, looking truly human and joyful for the first time in the film; Sandra as dutiful daughter Amy)--are reunited in a touching scene. And although Michael may still be handcuffed to his briefcase, he is no longer chained to his money, the case's contents of 500,000 dollars having been scattered all over the airport floor. The 360-degree pan now reasserts itself for the third and final time as the camera swoops and circles around the tearful duo, who are locked in an emotional hug. The camera movement here differs from the previous pans in two significant ways. Where the other pans moved clockwise, this one has the camera move in the opposite direction, suggesting (as in CARRIE) a disruption of the natural order of time, but here with positive results. With Michael and Sandra's past-oriented obsessions now conclusively broken for both characters, we may reasonably assume that having regained their past love, they will now be able to live fully in the present.

In the two previous scenes with pans the camera was a dispassionate, unemotional observer (as dispassionate and unemotional as the film's two principals). Now, with the clock turned back to the last time that Michael and Amy were truly happy (the engagement party when Michael, holding his daughter in his arms, waltzed her around the room), the camera can reflect their dual joy at being freed of their past obsessions and reunited in the present in a lovely resurrection of their original courtly dance. Here, though, it is the camera itself that does a little dance, panning not once but over and over again, and stopping with a shot that shows us father and daughter in a tearful embrace, happy again after all of those miserable years. Michael has bought back his daughter with his emotions, with his true, selfless love.[7] We leave them locked together on screen in a freeze-frame icon of devotion and trust.

NOTES

1. See The Monthly Film Bulletin, October, 1976, p. 217.
2. The plot is an obvious borrowing from Hitchcock's VER-
   TIGO, although only the essentials of the earlier film
   are here employed. Doubling is, naturally, the main
   structural element in the film: two kidnappings, two
   ransoms, two look-alike wives, two partners. In fact,
   the title of the production was originally Double Ransom, itself suitably ambiguous since "double" may refer to the two attempts at ransoming or the attempts
   to ransom the two Courtlands: Elizabeth and Amy.
3. Albert J. La Valley, ed. Focus on Hitchcock. Engle-
   wood Cliffs, N.J.: Prentice-Hall, 1972.
4. It is regrettable that the implied theme of incest in the
   film is not more fully developed. Sex between Michael
   and Sandra is sidestepped by the latter's assertion that
   Michael will, until they are married, have to be understanding, since she is "a good girl." One wonders,
   though, if no passionate kissing or petting occurred between them.
5. Perhaps no clearer indication of Michael's shallowness
   exists than the fact that, reflecting his personality,
   the script of OBSESSION (unlike that for any other
   De Palma film) is curiously devoid of humor.
6. Edgar Allan Poe. Selected Writings, ed. Edward David-
   son. Boston: Houghton Mifflin Co., 1956.
7. The emotional scene between Michael and Amy easily ex-
   ceeds that exhibited between Michael and Elizabeth, a
   further hint at the incestuous desires between father
   and daughter.

Chapter Five: "AFTER THE BLOOD COME THE BOYS"

In theme and treatment, CARRIE remains De Palma's masterpiece to this point. Nowhere else in the director's films does such total agreement exist between the message that a film carries and the manner in which that message is communicated through dialogue, acting, editing, and camerawork. Although the film may in certain senses be regarded as a derivative of PSYCHO, it can also be seen as so curiously characteristic of De Palma (with the emphasis on an examination of sex and various "powers") that it is safe to classify CARRIE as a virtually pure and indigenous work.

While a later De Palma film like THE FURY employs telekinesis as a character personality trait, CARRIE is the film in which De Palma fully realized that a character's power may be used to represent both an extrasensory force and a manipulative tool that is employed to influence the actions of others.

One need only point out the distinctions between CARRIE's source--the novel by Stephen King--and the film to see how in the transfer to the screen the story has been significantly improved. King's novel can be reduced to a series of quick descriptions. We have Carrie, the young girl with telekinetic ability; her evangelist mother; her schoolmates (Sue Snell and Tommy, Chris Hargenson and Billy). The basic action in both book and film is roughly the same--Carrie is made the butt of a cruel joke by Chris and Billy, and visits revenge on virtually the entire high school senior class at its

50

The quintessential De Palma image: Sissy Spacek in the blood
baptism from CARRIE.

year-end prom--although the film expands the scope of the
book's characterizations and scenes. The film ends with the
destruction of Carrie's house and Sue Snell's nightmare, while
the book lingers on beyond Carrie's demise, and does not
contain Sue's enlightening dream, which acts as such a successful closure device in the film.

King's book is poorly written (with sketchy characterization and awkward dialogue) and rather unconvincing. The
addition of a framing device (in the form of medical reports
on "the Carrie White syndrome") only further distances the
hastily-drawn figure of Carrie from the reader.

The film improves upon its source material by portraying Carrie (Sissy Spacek) as a sympathetic figure, making
it clear that "the power" is more stigma than saving grace.
Already alienated from her schoolmates (she apparently has
no friends and with her shy, reserved manner, is easy prey
for practical jokes and snide comments), she is further dis-
tanced from them by this new difference that has descended
upon her. At home, she is victimized by her mother (Piper
Laurie), for whom she is apparently a constant reminder of
sin (the child as a product of the procreative act; as Mrs.
White preaches to Carrie, "the first sin was intercourse")
and a receptacle for the "religion" that Mrs. White (judging
by her one proselytizing scene, with Sue's mother) unsuccess-
fully promulgates through town. The added attribute of the
power further alienates mother and daughter, with Mrs. White
believing her daughter's ability to be Satanically-derived.[1]

As is usual in horror films (from which CARRIE borrows various conventions and, as in the nighttime thunder-
claps and lightning accompanying her announcement about attending the Prom, gently parodies them as well), the scene
in which "the power" is invested in the individual (like the
creation of the monster in the Frankenstein series, or the
significant scenes in THE WEREWOLF involving the transfer
of the curse) is given a great deal of thematic significance.
The first sign in CARRIE of the girl's telekinetic ability occurs during the scene in which she is showering at school.
Complemented by the romantic, lilting strains of Pino Donaggio's music, the slow-motion camera snakes its way through
the girls' locker room, elevating the female students' carous-
ing while half-dressed to the level of movements imbued with
grace, as though the spectator were secretly glimpsing a
group of nymphs at play. At the end of the locker room
tracking shot, De Palma cuts to Carrie in the shower. The

slow motion technique's lyrical effects, combined with the
suggestiveness of the nude Carrie and the way in which her
hands--soaping her body--linger over her breasts and left
thigh (the latter faces the camera, thereby barely conceal-
ing her pubic hair), all contribute to the feeling of mild sexual excitation that is created here.

It is at the high point of this section that, after a final thigh caress by Carrie, we are shown the thick stream
of blood that comes coursing down her leg as a result of
what we learn is her first menstruation. Almost immediately,
De Palma jars the viewer by cutting to a regular motion shot,
with Carrie discovered screaming in fear.   Unaware of what
a menstrual cycle is (her mother has never discussed sex
with her), Carrie believes that this bleeding will lead to her
death (a conclusion that, given the inexorability of the film's
events, is, ironically, correct). Rather than receiving any
sympathy from her classmates, though, she in instead taunted
and reviled. The other girls (at Chris Hargenson's behest)
begin to pelt her with tampons in a mock stoning of the innocent, while they scream "plug it up, plug it up."

In the midst of this action, and after the arrival of
Miss Collins (Betty Buckley), the gym teacher, the telekinetic
power asserts itself. Carrie screams and, immediately thereafter, an overhead lightbulb bursts. Two inferences can be
drawn from this chain of events. First, the simultaneous on-
set of menstruation and "the power" strongly suggests that the
two forces are either linked or, more likely, are involved in
some pattern of causality. Second, Carrie is pointedly made
to feel that her bleeding between the legs (which, at this
point, is all that the event can mean to her) is involved not
only with fear, revilement, and alienation, but with death as
well. The fact that, to appropriate the film's slang-ridden
parlance, the power first manifests itself along with "the
curse" suggests that the power itself is a curse, a view sup-
ported by the film's subsequent events.

With an initial traumatizing experience like this occurring during the first menstruation, it is safe to conclude that
without immediate comfort and an explanation of what has happened, Carrie will, regardless of subsequent rationalizations,
always at least subconsciously associate this event with a
stigma every time it happens. The offscreen interlude after
Miss Collins' entrance into the locker room and before her
appearance along with Carrie in the principal's office is involved (as we learn from Miss Collins' discussion with the

principal) with her explaining the menstruation and its significance to Carrie.   Nevertheless, the element of uneasi-
ness, and the suggested revulsion at female sexuality attending it, immediately returns in the form of the principal's obvious distaste at the sight of Carrie's menstrual blood on
Miss Collins' shorts.   Nor is Carrie's anxiety in any way
alleviated by the principal's repeated mispronouncement of
her name (he calls her "Cassie" at least three times), a
mistake that results in the second manifestation of Carrie's
power which, as in its first appearance, ends in destruction.
This time, the principal's ashtray is flung to the floor.

On the way home from school, Carrie avails herself
of the power's destructive element, causing a young boy who
is taunting her to skid off his bicycle, hurting his knee.
(The boy is not only riding circles around her, but also reminding her of her alienation by calling her "crazy Carrie,
crazy Carrie").   Thus at this point, at least unconsciously,
Carrie realizes that her new power may be used to avenge
herself on those who cause her pain.   When we recall that
similar methods of manipulative revenge are used by all of
the film's major characters (who use sex as a tool to get
others to do what they want), and that Carrie's power is already strongly associated with the sexual urge, we can see
how even this early in the film CARRIE's main themes are
already fairly well established.

The escape to the home, a place that one would con-
ventionally regard as a source of refuge, instead becomes
for the beleaguered girl a penetration into the very center
of revulsion and horror about the nature of sex and power.
As soon as Carrie enters the house, Margaret White--already
informed by Miss Collins about the events at school--smacks
Carrie over the head with a thick evangelical text and forces
her to her knees.   She then turns to a chapter titled "The
Sins of Woman," starts to preach to her about "the curse of
blood" (an apt phrase given the film's later events), and
makes her repeat the phrase "Eve was weak."   Thus, the
lesson that sex equals pain (Mrs. White's physical abuse of
her daughter) and death (the taste of the forbidden fruit that
Eve offered to Adam "brought death into the world, and all
our woe, with loss of Eden[ic]" naïvete,[2] as in the brief innocence of the shower scene sacrificed to the curse of sex)
is again impressed upon Carrie.   Mrs. White's domination
over her daughter and her manipulation of the poor girl--first
by keeping her ignorant of sex, then, in a classic double bind,
punishing her for having gained "knowledge" of it--only further
affirm the view of sex as power that the film propounds.

For Carrie, the home is thus the source of corruption and evil. The scene concludes with Carrie's return to an enclosed place (the closet, like the shower stall, offers no escape; Mrs. White locks the former, the students block the exit from the latter) in which she must somehow (in the school through washing, here through cleansing by prayer) attempt to divest herself of sex's stain.

CARRIE's following scenes expand upon our understanding of these characters and their dilemmas. Margaret White is seen calling on Sue Snell's mother who, even early in the afternoon, is having a drink (presumably alcoholic given the toast she offers) and watching a television soap opera (whose soundtrack indicates that it is presently dealing with a wronged wife who was unaware that her presumably philandering husband had "been in Chicago"; corruption seems to be rampant in the film's universe) at the same time as she is talking on the telephone. Apparently, we are to view Mrs. Snell as representative of the town's traditional parents: middle class, with nothing better to do in the afternoon than drink, watch television, and gossip. With Margaret White's arrival at her door (Mrs. Snell sees her coming and wishes for an escape), an obvious contrast is set up between the two female types. Mrs. Snell is relaxed, casually dressed, and idle; her hair is coiffed and she is indulging herself. Mrs. White is obsessive and high-strung, dressed in a billowy dress that seems like the formal attire of a priestess, and busy on her rounds; her hair is worn natural and loose and she preaches self-abnegation. Neither character seems like an attractive role model to base one's behavior on; the conformist seems without purpose, the purposeful outsider is clearly a fanatic.

The women disagree on the state of their children. Mrs. White says that children today are "wandering through the wilderness of sin," which tempts them, and that "these are godless times." Mrs. Snell replies that her Sue "is a good girl." Nothing in the short scene so tellingly communicates the contrast between the two women as Mrs. White's comment that the world is going to ruin, and Mrs. Snell's rejoinder ("I'll drink to that") which unwittingly indicates a desire to toast moral degradation.

The polarized world of CARRIE, in which a Manichean struggle continually exists between good and evil, is represented most directly by the two couples to whom we are then introduced: Sue Snell (Amy Irving) and Tommy Ross (William Katt), Chris Hargenson (Nancy Allen) and Billy Nolan (John

Travolta).   Again, we are treated to personality and visual
contrasts of a most striking nature.   Sue and Tommy are
quiet and demure; they are attending and participating in
classes, and both are involved in extracurricular activities
(Sue works on the Senior Prom committee; Tommy is a
baseball and football star).   Chris, on the other hand, is
never seen within the hallways or classrooms of the school
(we do see her briefly in the gymnasium, though) and is apparently only working on the Prom committee to revenge
herself on Carrie, while Billy doesn't seem to attend school
at all.   One need only point to the contrast between Tommy's
blond halo-head of hair and Billy's greasy dark mop, and the
differences between Sue's natural lips and regulation gym
shorts and Chris's bee-stung kisser and suggestive, designer-
styled track togs to realize the distinctions between the couples.   Sue and Tommy are, at least on the surface, among
the town's good children.   Career-oriented and conscientious,
they are never glimpsed doing anything more intimate than
holding hands.   Chris and Billy, though, are portrayed as
crude (their language is rife with words like "crap" and
"shit"), unprincipled (they will do virtually anything to shame
Carrie), and engaged in explicit sexual provocation (exemplified by Chris's lack of a brassiere and the breathy way
she sidles up to Billy in the car).   Action for contrasting
action (the two couples' scenes are edited to produce the
impression of matched opposites), these characters under-
score the polarized nature of the film's universe.   Even the
school staff involved with Carrie divide into matched doubles:
on the one hand, the unsympathetic principal (Mr. Morton)
plus the sarcastic English teacher (Mr. Fromm), and on the
other, the well-intentioned gym teacher, Miss Collins.   Despite their differences, though, all three are equally responsible for hurting Carrie and are thus killed off at the film's
end.

     In CARRIE, the forces of good are shown to be clearly
unequal to the task of combating evil.   The apparently lauda-
ble impulse behind Tommy's accompanying Carrie to the prom
(it first seems that Sue encourages him to take the girl in an
attempt to socialize Carrie) not only sets the stage for the
holocaust at the dance, but also creates the conditions that
give rise to the practical joke that Chris and Billy play on
Carrie.   Miss Collins must also be blamed for Carrie's appearance at the prom.   Her efforts at "bringing Carrie out"
by pep-talking her into using make-up and styling her hair
can, in the context of the film's implicit condemnation of
artifice and design in sexuality, be criticized as encouraging

Carrie to participate in sexual dissembling, a kind of Eve-like temptation.[3] Nor are the traditional enforcers of the public moral code portrayed as effective. The police who cruise by Billy's car and shine a flashlight on him fail to see the can of beer he is (apparently illegally) drinking from, even though they are looking directly at him.

The view of sexuality that CARRIE adopts and pro-pounds is not the "normal, well-adjusted" view of parents like Mrs. Snell and couples like Sue and Tommy, but that of Carrie's mother, for whom sex is the gate to hell and damnation and in whose view "sin never dies." Margaret White's impassioned recounting of her relationship with her husband--in which at the beginning they "remained clean" un-til he returned one night "with the roadhouse liquor on his breath and took me"--reveals an admixture of both fascina-tion with sex ("and I liked it, I liked it") and revulsion over it (thus her agonized expression when describing how her husband "put it in me" and her assertion that, presumably during menstruation, the boys can "smell it on you").

Although we may regard Mrs. White's ministry as her (somewhat unnatural) means of sublimating her sexuality, we must also admit that her polarized view of good and evil and her corrupt, conservative, biblical reading of sex as leading only to damnation, are confirmed by the film's events. From Carrie's first menstruation, down through her involvement with Tommy (touchingly replete with timidity and nervous glances, and culminated by the moving pas de deux at the prom), the destruction of much of the senior class, the pen-etration/impalement of Mrs. White (whose groans at death are so suggestively sexual) and Carrie's own death, the film confirms that sex is death, and that the reproductive round almost inevitably leads to destruction.[4]

What is so striking about CARRIE is the manner in which sex is also portrayed as a power that thus invites com-parison with the film's other power (itself sexually related): telekinesis. The shower scene affirms this view, as do the scenes in which Chris and Sue get their respective men to do what they want. Both women employ sexual favors; char-acteristically, Sue (the "good girl") manipulates Tommy by denying him her sexual presence (she does her homework in-stead) while Chris (the "bad" girl) influences Billy by fellating him.[5] (One should also note that since, as we have seen, Carrie's power is sexually derived, and is used by her throughout the film for various purposes, she too, may be said to use sex to attain what she wants.)

Top: The family pietà--redemption (the upward look for in-
spiration) and retribution (the downward-pointing knife) here
combine. Bottom: The impalement of Margaret White (Piper
Laurie).

The film's language--both verbal and visual--confirms and complements these attitudes. The dialogue is filled with references to sexuality: "come" is the word used most often, usually in intentionally ambiguous ways. Mrs. White's speech to Carrie about "after the blood come the boys" puns on the significance of "come," drawing upon meanings of both pursuit (the boys seek out, come after, the blood as though sexual maturity in itself were sufficient cause for attraction between the sexes, a world view of constantly rutting bodies in heat) and temporality (after a woman's sexual maturity, the attracted boys can achieve ejaculation through sex with her). Her repeated statement on the night of the prom that Tommy will not arrive to pick up Carrie ("he's not going to come; he's not coming") is ironically prophetic in view of the unrealized sexual relationship between the two young people.

The pig that Billy kills to provide blood for Carrie's dousing at the prom establishes a link between Carrie and the animal. It is clear that Carrie's dousing with blood at the dance is a significant repetition of her first blood baptism in the school shower, with the differences that the shame now occurs before the whole senior class, while the "innocents" to be slaughtered at the second baptism are the students themselves, not Carrie. The oppressed is thus revenged on her oppressors.

Clearly, the pig's blood baptism is a public confirmation of Satan's primacy and an inversion of Margaret White's ministerial pronouncements about "God's salvation through Christ's blood" (what Carrie receives is Satan's damnation through the devil's--pig's--blood). The use of the pig as the source of the blood makes more comprehensible both the statement that Chris makes to Carrie at the film's beginning after Carrie flubs a volleyball serve ("You eat shit") and the painted-on message that is barely glimpsed being washed off the gym wall while Miss Collins berates her charges for their treatment of the girl ("Carrie White eats shit"). The pig is a ruminating animal that occasionally ingests its own feces; thus, Chris's two statements (we can assume that the painted message is hers) link Carrie with the pig, the cloven-hoofed one, the devil. However, it is Chris who is portrayed as the film's real pig/devil (in teen slang, she is a "pig" in that she flaunts her sexuality and a "devil" in that she maliciously attempts to prepare the way for her rival's demise).[6] Like a true devil, she cannot abide good in any form; and Satan-like, she tempts the pseudo-Christ Carrie[7] with worldly fame (Carrie submits to having her name on the ballot for

Prom Queen), only to be foiled and thrown down in the end (her death and Billy's seem the only "righteous" murders in the film).

The Christ/Satan dichotomy continually reappears in CARRIE, always as an integral part of the action. The rock song being performed when Carrie and Tommy enter the prom hall contains a lyric about "the devil got a hold of her soul,"[8] which reminds us of Margaret White's earlier ominous warning about the source of her daughter's telekinetic ability ("that's Satan's power; he doesn't let you know he's working through you.")[9]

Later, Carrie and Tommy vote for themselves as Prom King and Queen (placing their mark on the ballot with a significant cross, on which the camera carefully zooms in), over Carrie's initial protest. Encouraged by Tommy, Carrie has agreed to the voting (thereby contributing to her own undoing), stating "to the Devil (with modesty)," a prophetic statement (thus making her a true daughter of seer Margaret White) in light of the girl's essential innocence, which is soon to be shattered by Chris's Satanically-cruel trick.

The cut at this point to a shot of Margaret White pacing about her kitchen table establishes further linkages as we see that Margaret has crossed two utensils in the middle of the table (thus producing a shape identical in configuration and intended function to the painted cross in the street fronting her house) in order to ward off evil. Both exorcistic gestures prove ineffectual, though, since in spite of the cross in the street Tommy does arrive to take Carrie to the ill-fated prom, while all of the kitchen utensil-related cleansings (the mock-castration of Tommy as Margaret chops a carrot with the same knife that later she will use to stab Carrie and wave over her while she makes the sign of the cross) do nothing to prevent both Carrie and Margaret from being delivered into evil.

Even Tommy, in a unusual burst of prophecy only hinted at in his plagiarized (and thereby corruptly obtained) poem about sexual hypocrisy, gives voice to visions, ambiguously asking Carrie after she verbally interrupts him, "would you let me finish?" The word "finish" links up with Margaret White's statement about Tommy's "not coming," both of which assertions are seen to be true given the brevity of his relationship with Carrie. Later, after the descent of the pig's blood, Tommy silently mouths the words "what the Hell?," thereby correcting (albeit inadvertently) identifying the Satanic source of Chris's revenge. [10]

     The cinematography in CARRIE is one of the strongest and most successful communicators of the film's meanings. Among the various symbolic camera movements that De Palma uses to reinforce the scenario's meanings are numerous downward and upward crane shots, suggestive of degradations and ironic moral and spiritual ascents. The film begins with an overhead crane shot; the camera slowly descends into the midst of the girls' volleyball game in which Carrie and Chris are participating. This move into the action--a traditional opening device in films--hints at an immersion in ordinary events that is belied by the film's action. Instead, one can view this initial descent as the beginning of the spiritual descent in the next sequence in which the downward flow of Carrie's menstrual blood signals degradation for the girl, as do Chris's "going down" on Billy[11] and the slow-motion descent of the pig's blood at the prom, the latter presaging Carrie's last descent: her death in a telekinetically-collapsed house. [12]

     While movements down toward debasement and degradation are prevalent in CARRIE, upward movements--traditionally connoting spiritual ascension or idealism--are, when they occur, portrayed ironically. To take the prime example: when, in the film's last scene, De Palma reverses the opening shot's camera movement by pulling up and away from a shot of Sue and her mother we are, in spite of the camera movement, left with the impression that this ascent away from the film's terrors is impossible. As Sue's dream indicates, rising above one's degradations is impossible.

     Perhaps the most significant camerawork in the film is that employed during the dance between Tommy and Carrie. The entire scene is redolent with idealization and realized aspirations; for Carrie, the night is magical.

     When Carrie and Tommy rise to dance, the camera first follows them at eye level and then, as the dance continues and becomes more amorous (culminating in their first kiss, a kiss that Tommy sincerely offers), the camera slowly cranes downward, tilting up to look at them and thus elevating the two characters to a position connoting power and predominance that is at variance with their eventual helplessness. While at this point Carrie and Tommy may feel uplifted by their circumstances and surroundings, they are soon to be cast down as they are helplessly involved in the film's fateful events.

The most significant aspect of this sequence occurs after De Palma's virtually invisible cut at the beginning of Tommy and Carrie's dance, during which actors William Katt and Sissy Spacek were placed on a revolving floor platform to accentuate the dizzying swirl of emotions that the dance occasions for the characters they are portraying. The floor piece turns clockwise, so that Tommy and Carrie--with their romantic hopes being realized--turn in the accustomed, natural direction of clocks, as though they are in harmonious synchronism with time. The camera, though--communicating as always the true movement of the plot and its tendencies towards doom--at the same time turns counter-clockwise, in essence throwing the "time out of joint" and setting up a disarming tension between the way that the characters would like things to occur and the way that inevitability, here represented by the camerawork, intends to operate.

In this sequence one can see the camera taking on the aspects of a film character, probing into the recesses of the film's meanings (as it also does in the next scene when it traces the trip rope from its actuator, Chris, to its object, the pig's blood, a movement repeated later from Sue's point of view). In this sense, and in his use of the dispassionate god's eye shot from above (the high crane shot over the gym floor looking down on Chris and her friend Norma as they discuss the plot against Carrie; the merciless observation from above of Sue's nightmare fit at the film's end), one can see De Palma establishing linkages with the Hitchcock film most notable for its camera-as-character movements: PSYCHO. Moreover, the relationship between Carrie and her mother mirrors the one between Norman and Mrs. Bates, with suggestive elements of parent-child sexual rivalry and an overall examination of repression being primary characteristics of each film's scenario. Additionally, one should not overlook the "screeching violin" sounds that accompany Margaret White's impalement with daggers resembling the one that Norman wields. Such sounds are an obvious homage to the Hitchcock film, although less flattering to the original than the previous example concerning characterization because they appear more as a direct borrowing than an adaptation or reworking of material.

CARRIE's last two scenes have evoked much deserved comment, although discussion of them has in general failed to integrate their meanings into the film's total scenario. Immediately after the destruction of Carrie, her mother, and their house, De Palma cuts to a scene showing Sue Snell, carrying a bouquet of flowers, calmly walking down a street. The fact that the sequence is in slow motion should give us some clue to its unusual character, since only the shower scene and Queen of the Prom sequences were shot in this manner and both, as we know, ended in disaster. Recalling these previous scenes, we are thus somewhat prepared for the point in the present sequence at which Sue, in placing the flowers on Carrie's grave (which is marked with a white cross, appropriate for the pure-aspiring Carrie White), is grabbed from below by Carrie's blood-stained hand, which thrusts through the rocks covering the grave and clutches Sue in its grip. (Judging by the film's next scene, we may justifiably read this action as demonstrating Carrie's strong "hold" or influence on Sue, even beyond the girl's death). At this juncture, the scene reverts to regular speed as Sue tries to release herself. The following scene match-cuts to Sue writhing in her bed. The action has been a dream; her mother vainly tries to comfort her and--in a mirror image of the film's opening crane-down shot--the camera coolly pulls up and away.

Sue's (Amy Irving) dream towards CARRIE's end: the revenge of "the innocent" on "the innocent."

The scene with Sue walking toward the grave is unusual for two reasons. In terms of technique, it should be
noted that the entire sequence was shot in reverse, with Amy
Irving walking backwards while a wind machine blew her gown
and hair from in front of her so that when projected forwards
the scene would show her walking normally, with the wind
wafting her hair and gown behind her. What clues the viewer
into the scene's unusual nature is not only the somewhat contrived manner of the girl's forward walk, but a barely
glimpsed car in the background, which can be seen moving
backwards down a side street. As in the prom dance sequence, the camera work inverts the normal order, affirming at the film's end, despite Carrie's death, that the time
is still out of joint. The moral order has been ruptured,
and continues to manifest its disturbances through Carrie's
misguided but well-intentioned silent friend, Sue.

Throughout CARRIE, we have seen how inversion of
traditional expectations--expectations with respect to good's
traditional triumph over evil, normal versus corrupt attitudes
about sexual behavior--have, to employ a physical phrase,
been elevated over their opposites. In this penultimate sequence, inversion (here manifested as reversal) is once again
present: Evil has triumphed (Mrs. White's view of sex as
leading to death and damnation, and Chris's view of sex as
essentially dirty and forbidden, have been borne out by the
film's events); Carrie and Sue's attempts to act in opposition
to these views have failed. The world is thus unhinged.
Satan reigns, so that in Sue's dream the Carrie White she
sympathized with has become the corrupt Carrie White of
the townspeople's view: a devil, an evil influence, a curse.
Thus the inscription on Carrie's cross ("Carrie White burns
in Hell"), thus Carrie's return from the grave to remind Sue
that she will never be free of corruption's taint.

Is there, then, a resurrection from Hell for those
damned, as seems apparent in the dream? Is Carrie's pig/
devil influence still in operation? Apparently, yes. The
Carrie who became sociable suffered as a result, and annihilated Tommy, Billy, Chris, Miss Collins (appropriately
crushed by a basketball backboard), the principal who repeatedly mispronounced her name, the English teacher who
belittled her comments about Tommy's poem, and--judging
by Mrs. Snell's remark ("the funerals--with Tommy and all
the others gone")--much of the (Norman?) Bates High School
Senior class, lives again through the person of Sue Snell, the
"good girl" who was so significantly involved in setting in mo-

tion the chain of events that led to such horrors. Thus, the
Margaret White gospel of sex as evil, of sex as a curse, is
not only borne out by the film's events, but is seen to apply
to everyone (Sue, Tommy, Chris, Billy, Miss Collins, Carrie, even--despite her renunciation of sex--Margaret herself)
regardless of their good intentions or the way they lead their
lives. At CARRIE's end, it is not God who triumphs, but
Satan. Carrie burns in Hell, and Sue is there with her forever in her dreams, which reveal the true depravity underlying everything. The blood of the lamb is replaced in the
film's world by the blood of Satan/the pig, in which (considering corruption's pervasiveness) we are all baptized. In
CARRIE, the entire universe is bathed in the blood of the
pig, and no amount of penance will ever remove its stain.

NOTES

1. In fact, after seeing a manifestation of her daughter's
    power, Margaret White not only calls Carrie a "witch"
    and compares her to the devil, but has Carrie inad-
    vertently admit that she is, in a sense, herself the
    fallen angel. "It [making things move] is nothing to
    do with Satan," she says. "It's me." This linkage,
    reaffirmed throughout the film, is repeated towards
    CARRIE's end when Margaret White refers to her
    daughter's return to their house with the phrase, "and
    now the Devil has come home." Covered as she is
    with the blood of the pig (as opposed to "the blood of
    the lamb" that Margaret White sings to herself about),
    and fresh from the slaughter at the Prom, Carrie cer-
    tainly seems to fit the part.
2. John Milton, Paradise Lost.
3. Visual affirmation of this linkage among Carrie's peers--
    be they well-intentioned or not--is provided at two im-
    portant points in the film. Walking behind the bleach-
    ers at the school track, Sue and Tommy discuss Sue's
    plan to have her boyfriend take Carrie to the Prom.
    The scene chillingly foreshadows a later scene featur-
    ing another couple--Chris and Billy--who, partially ob-
    scured, are glimpsed behind the bleacher-like slats
    of the stairs leading up to the Senior Prom stage.
        During the Prom sequence, we see Chris holding
    onto the rope that will release the pig's blood and then
    are shown Sue (in precisely the same physical position
    as Chris) standing near the stage with her hands vir-
    tually touching another portion of the rope as though

she, too, were in some sense going to release the
blood (which, given the fact that she is, along with
Miss Collins, equally responsible for Carrie's attending the dance, is quite true). Finally, De Palma completes the ironic female triumvirate by following these
two adjacent shots with a view of Miss Collins, thereby
suggesting that all three women are strongly involved
in Carrie's undoing.

Moreover, each character's desire to have Carrie
attend the dance stems from what must be viewed as
reprehensible hubris. Sue wants Carrie to go to the
Prom so that she atone for her participation in the
girl's locker room revilement. "I asked [Tommy] to
[take her] because I thought I owed it to Carrie," she
says, but it seems more likely that she felt she owed
it to herself to make up for her immature actions.
Chris wants Carrie at the Prom to shame her, thereby
undoubtedly expiating some of her discomfort over her
"fallen" status, a status made more apparent when
contrasted with what she perceives as Carrie's "purity." Miss Collins--judging from De Palma's zooming
in on actress Betty Buckley's face to the exclusion of
Sissy Spacek while Miss Collins delivers reasons why
Carrie should go to the dance (she later ironically refers to the event as a night "you'll never forget")--is
clearly more interested in re-enacting through Carrie
her own special Prom night from years before (she
specifically mentions the event to Carrie at the Prom).
The fact that Sue, after discovering Chris and Billy
under the Prom stage, is ignorantly waylaid by Miss
Collins, only further contributes to the teacher's cul-
pability in the night's events. However, it must also
be admitted that had it not been for Miss Collins' interference (which results in Sue's expulsion from the
gym), Sue would have perished along with the other
students. Miss Collins has saved her from death, but
as CARRIE's end makes plain, she has also helped to
deliver her into a living hell.

4. If any further confirmation were needed of Margaret
    White's prophetic powers, one need only recall her
    insistence to Carrie that the students at the Prom are
    "all going to laugh at you," a vision whose truth is,
    unfortunately, ultimately realized.

    One should also note that through the actions of her
    daughter, Margaret White's self-expressed desired end
    ("I should have killed myself when he [her husband] put
    it in me") is finally achieved (knowledge of sexuality

destroys both mother and child). To complement the
assumption of a religious death, De Palma at this
point has Piper Laurie groan during her agony so that
her passion--itself an appropriately ambiguous word
to use here given its spiritual and physical meanings
--is replete with sounds that suggest sexual satisfaction. In death, truly, Margaret White thus melds the
film's two worlds, the religious and the physical, the
(traditionally) sacred and profane, ironically suggesting that in the end she attains a significant unity of
the polarities that throughout the film threaten to tear
her apart.

5. After the English teacher somewhat maliciously ridicules
Carrie's comment that Tommy's poem (about illicit
versus 'free' love) is "beautiful," Tommy curses the
teacher by muttering "you suck," thus recalling for
us the fellatio that Chris performed on Billy.

6. Further linkage between the pig-as-animal and pig-like
humans is provided in Billy's reference to Chris (during one of their arguments) as "you pig" and Freddy's
comment at the stockyard (where the pig is slaughtered
to provide blood for Carrie's ritualistic slaying) about
the mural ("Look at all those painted pigs. I went
out with the girl that posed for them; she was a real
pig."), a comment that not only compares women to
pigs but also--in its reference to "painted pigs"--re-
calls Chris's painted lips and Carrie's jaunt at the
drugstore where, in trying on various shades of lip-
stick, she unknowingly emulates her enemy.

We are also given dialogue evidence that not only
Chris and Billy (with their already-mentioned "crap"-
and "shit"-laden conversations) but Carrie's female
classmates as well are pig-like in their obsession
with low desires (sex, humiliation of others). Thus,
Miss Collins' significant use of the phrase "a real
shitty thing" to refer to the girls' taunting of Carrie.

If one doubts the significance of CARRIE's language,
one need only consider the PG-rated version of the film
that plays on commercial television. The "Carrie
White eats shit" wall slogan completely disappears;
Tommy's muttered taunt ("you suck") to the English
teacher is changed to "you're sick;" while Freddy's
use of a female term ("you pussy"--femininity thus
seen as the ultimate insult, an attitude close to that
of Margaret White's, who believes in Eve's weakness
and "the curse of blood") to tease Billy is reduced to
a simple "aw you."

The fights between Billy and Chris are similarly robbed of both symbolic significance and verbal power. The looped-in word "jerk" is substituted for "shit"; thus, Chris calls Billy "a stupid jerk" instead of the "stupid shit" of the film's R-rated version. Similarly, Miss Collins' phrase "a real shitty thing" becomes "a real nasty thing." The overall effect of such censoring is to virtually destroy the film's linguistic allusiveness.

7.   Ultimately, though, the film never consistently establishes Carrie's true status. She remains an ambiguous figure, Christ-like, victimized by most of her peers and her mother but Satanic as well in her use of her powers to get what she wants (telekinetically repulsing Mrs. White when her mother tries to prevent her from going to the Prom), gain revenge (the deaths of the Prom attendees and, later, Chris and Billy), or right apparent wrongs (as in her initial defense against Margaret White's sacrificial attack with a knife, a defense which--once she perceives it as unjustifiable-- is compensated for by her penitential death, not at her mother's hands, but by her own).

We may, nevertheless, regard the manner in which the girl dispatches her mother as an act of ironic kindness. By telekinetically manipulating various kitchen utensils, she first has Margaret White stabbed through the right hand and pinned to the molding of the kitchen doorway with the triangular (cf. SISTERS and PSYCHO) blade that Mrs. White used against her. Then she has Mrs. White stabbed four more times-- once more in the hand (the left one, which is also pinned to the molding) and then three times in the body (once to the heart, twice to the abdomen). The positions of the wounds, the shape of the instruments causing them, and the martyr-like position that the dead Margaret White finally assumes (eyes open, head inclined to the viewer's left) precisely duplicate the physical attitude of the statue of St. Sebastian (like Margaret White, a proselytizer who refused to quit preaching and was, as a result, executed) in the closet where Mrs. White locks Carrie to pray. Unwittingly, in the act of protecting herself and murdering Mrs. White, Carrie has apotheosized her mother. Mrs. White's martyrdom (complemented by the soundtrack's swelling organ music refrain) is not without its poignancy.

8.   This isn't the only musical tag that provides a clue to a

sequence's meanings. The scene with Chris and Billy
in which Chris blatantly uses sex to involve her boy-
friend in the plot against Carrie opens with Martha
and the Vandellas' "Heat Wave" (a high-voltage song
about passion) playing on the soundtrack.

Additionally, one should note the tender ballads
used as background music at the Prom when Carrie,
Tommy, and Miss Collins talk and, later, when Carrie and Tommy dance. Both songs ("Born to Have It
All" and "I Never Dreamed That Someone Like You
Could Love Someone Like Me") complement the sweet
lyricism of these sequences.

9.   Carrie's answer to her mother's claim that "(Satan) entered your father and carried him off" clearly points
up the distinction between Mrs. White's obsessively
religious interpretation of events and her daughter's
desire to see things in a secular light. Carrie states
in reply, "he ran away, momma, he ran away with a
woman; everybody knows that" (a statement interrupted
midway by Margaret White's barely audible hiss of the
words "Satan did it"). Unfortunately for Carrie, it is
her mother's point of view with respect to events that
is shown in the film to be the correct one.

The viewer should also note the film's color sym-
bolism, which visually clues us in to the differences
between mother and daughter. Mrs. White (the family name itself is an ironic mockery of the woman's
desire to appear pure although she has, as she herself admits, known sin; such knowledge is reflected in
her evangelist's robe's being black, not the expected
white), viewing her daughter's attendance at the Prom
as a symbolic fall into promiscuity, claims that the
girl's self-made Prom dress is "red. I might have
known it would be red." Carrie corrects her: "it's
pink, Momma," thereby rightly claiming for the gown
(and the carnations that Tommy has sent her) a color
that nicely mediates between white's symbolic purity
and red's symbolic passion. Once the pig's blood is
spilled on the girl, though, Mrs. White's vision is
realized, and the gown is truly red. Even after Carrie's purifying bath (which occurs after the blood-bath
at the Prom), the girl is again sullied--this time with
the blood from the wound that her mother inflicts on
her in an attempt to use blood (her daughter's) against
blood (the pig's, as a mark of Satan and the sin of
sex) in a final, albeit useless, act of purification.

Carrie's valiant bid for acceptable normalcy also

appears when Mrs. White, commenting on her daughter's appearance in the Prom dress, states, "everyone will see your filthy dugs." Carrie vainly tries to counter this debased view of sex in a statement ("breasts, Momma, they're called breasts, and every woman has them") that ironically damns all women to the same plight of pain, embarrassment, and anxiety that the film demonstrates as inevitable. Remembering at this point the way that Billy leered at Chris' breasts (unencumbered by a brassiere, and which he later appropriately refers to as "tits") in the car scene, one can see how all-pervasive CARRIE makes the view of sex as corrupt appear to be (the television version renders the reference meaningless by changing the word "tits" to "shirt").

10. Typical De Palma foreshadowings occur throughout CARRIE, setting up for us affirmations of the tragic ineluctability that is a trademark of De Palma's film universes. After Miss Collins tells her gym class about their punitive detention, Chris repeatedly states, "I'm not coming; I'm not going to come," an accurate remark since the only satisfaction we ever see her achieve is not a sexual one, but a pleasure derived from the joke she plays on Carrie.

After their violent encounter on the athletic field, Chris tells Miss Collins that "this isn't over by a long shot." The girl is quite right; their dispute will only be ended by the Prom night cataclysm.

In response to Miss Collins' accusation that Chris cannot leave the field since "the period's not up, Hargenson," Chris replies, "it is for me." Reading the word "period" as a reference to menstrual cycles (as in Sue's earlier statement to Miss Collins explaining the row in the locker room by saying that "Carrie's got her period"), one can--given her rapidly approaching demise--appreciate the accuracy of Chris's statement.

Later, after Billy executes a rapid swerve with his car, Chris asks him, "do you want to get us killed?" Appropriately, it is precisely after just such a swerve (the U-shaped, telekinetically-influenced one that veers Billy's car away from Carrie) that Chris and Billy die.

11. The action occurs in Billy's car in which, significantly, Chris and Billy are--as a result of Carrie's telekinesis--burned to death. The earlier "heat wave" reaches full temperature in the cataclysm, as the plot against Carrie, hatched in the car, is appropriately terminated

in the same vehicle in a fiery deluge. Martha and
the Vandellas' song ironically forecasts the event:
"love is like a heat wave, burning, burning, burning."

12. The house is also destroyed by a fire, one caused by
Carrie and doubtless inspired by her perceiving two
things: the purgative purpose behind her mother's
lighting all of the candles in the house (the religious
overtones of the gesture are successfully complemented by the organ music accompanying their discovery) and the significance of the two candles on the
bed (the seat of sexuality, the source of all of CAR-
RIE's ills) as symbols of the mother/daughter pair
who only through fire may escape the fires of both
passion and damnation. (The two candles, though,
have been seen before: on the dining room table as,
under the gaudy Last Supper tapestry, Carrie and her
mother ate dinner. The meal does indeed prove to
be their last supper together, since the Prom is soon
to follow; consequently, Margaret White's inadvertently
extinguishing the candles--when she throws the coffee
in Carrie's face--heralds a death for both mother and
daughter that will soon be realized).

  Although earlier "cleansings" in the film only resulted in shame and destruction (the locker room
shower sequence; the washing in pig's blood, the
post-Prom bathing), the impulse to free oneself of
evil taints through the use of baptismal water (the
fire hose at the Prom unleashes a stream of water
that breaks the neck of Chris's sneering friend, Norma, helps to electrocute the English teacher, Mr.
Fromm, and the principal, Mr. Morton, and--through
the resulting short-circuit--starts the fire that kills
off the rest of the students in the gym) and fire (the
gym conflagration, the immolation of Chris and Billy)
did prove productive. The ultimate destruction of
Carrie's house by fire completes the night's round of
sacrificial burnings.

With its theme of psychic forces at work in a self-aggrandizing universe within which there is no promise of redemption, THE FURY at first glance seems merely to extend the themes elucidated and examined so well in CARRIE two years earlier. Yet although the films are superficially similar, they are quite different with respect to the attitude that De Palma brings to the productions. THE FURY is recognizably a bigger, more expensive film than CARRIE, with a more ambitious theme to suit its larger budget and the presence of two costly star actors--Kirk Douglas and John Cassavetes-- to lend the project box-office sheen.

The contrasts with CARRIE are instructive. Where CARRIE was concerned with an outsider, a young girl alienated from her contemporaries in a small town, THE FURY places its telepathic others (Robin and Gillian) not only in the heart of great cities (Chicago and somewhere on the Riviera) but into the midst of political wheeling and dealing that we are meant to believe has global consequences. While CARRIE concerned itself with only one extrasensory individual, THE FURY has two, thus doubling the chances for De Palma to pepper the film with the kind of special effects set pieces he is so fond of. In contrast to CARRIE, THE FURY is less concerned with the alienating effects of mind powers on the individual than it is with the manner in which these powers may become co-opted by virtually invisible and apparently malicious forces: government agencies. True, sex and power are still linked in De Palma's mind; their

confluence is in evidence here. But THE FURY raises the
stakes over the earlier film by not only linking sex and power, but allying them with politics as well. The consequences
of the alliance are thus much more awesome.

This change in focus need not have resulted in a dim-
inution of sympathy for the victims of psychical power (Gillian and Robin), but it does. It must be admitted that De
Palma has never been very successful in building audience
identification with his films' characters. He achieved this
result in CARRIE, but that effect had less to do with his
direction of the film than with Sissy Spacek's exploitation of
her little-girl-lost look, her ability to use her pale, freckle-
faced beauty to win the audience over to her side. Moreover, CARRIE's script (by Lawrence D. Cohen) was clearly
biased in favor of Carrie's character, what with her repeated
victimizations, first by her schoolmates, then by her mother.
(In Carrie's view, even those who befriended her--including
Miss Collins and Tommy--abused her trust; had Sue Snell
remained at the prom, she too would doubtless have been
annihilated as well).

THE FURY's Amy Irving (who plays Gillian Bellaver)
does command the type of innocence that could elicit audience
sympathy, but overall the film fails to take advantage of it.
Instead, De Palma devotes the majority of screen time to de-
tailing the activities of Robin and Peter Sandza (Andrew Stevens and Kirk Douglas) and Childress (John Cassavetes). These
are, to be sure, interesting characters, but was it thereby
necessary to relegate the character of Gillian to the role of
a mere pawn? By doing so, De Palma unfortunately sacrifices any possible terror and suspense that we may feel concerning Gillian's entrapment and victimization. Apparently,
the director has yet to learn Hitchcock's lesson: terror is
increased when we care about a character and, consequently,
what is going to happen to him or her.

De Palma again borrows from Hitchcock the idea of
using paired actors--alike in associations and involvements
but with differing moral allegiances--to represent the polarized moralities in his political universe. We have the good
government agent (Peter Sandza) and the bad one (Childress);
the good psychic (Gillian) and her corrupted counterpart (Robin
Sandza). Finally, we are given the two female companions,
the one loyal and self-sacrificing (Carrie Snodgrass's Hester),
the other shrewd, calculating, looking out only for herself
(Fiona Lewis's Susan Charles). Such polarized characteriza-

tion suggests that THE FURY's view of politics is either extremely simplistic, overlooking conflicting allegiances combined in one character, or intentionally stylized for the sake of a dramatic exposition that (at least on the surface) never pretends to anything more than a fanciful representation of archetypal characters rather than people who appear to be "real." As the film's playful tone will reveal, the latter is obviously the case here.

While THE FURY may on one level be taken as making statements on power politics and the inevitable corruption within the political sphere of anyone who is not (like Peter Sandza) a totally free agent, it is also a film that blatantly manipulates its characters, putting them through the paces of a sprawling but entertaining series of near-escapes, occasional injuries (and a death or two), and psychic explosions, all designed for our amusement by the agent behind the whole proceedings: De Palma. Seen in this way, as a grand show to be enjoyed for its obvious staginess and various "acts," THE FURY is as much about filmmaking--the director's manipulation of his characters, the film's manipulation of audience reactions--as anything else.

Some critics--like Richard Combs in The Monthly Film Bulletin--have complained that THE FURY's plot is nothing more than the disposable frame upon which its grandiose scenes are hung. If this view were accurate, THE FURY would amount (at most) to no more than seven or eight minutes of "interesting" screen time, the remainder of the production merely serving as links between the special effects. How, then, to account for the entire film's entrancing effect? From its opening guerrilla attack to its closing cataclysm, THE FURY manages through sheer daring to keep the filmgoer fascinated, doing so because it employs consistent, unifying themes that justify De Palma's repeated attempts within the film to outdo himself.

THE FURY opens with Peter and Robin (and, for a time, Childress) seated at a beach-side table; they appear to be on holiday in the Mediterranean. As in the openings of CARRIE and OBSESSION, the universe we enter at the film's beginning is quite placid. Yet the feeling of calm thus created is almost immediately undermined by the cinematography. Instead of employing a static camera set up, De Palma has the camera pace back and forth around the table in disturbing, albeit graceful arcs; the smoothness of the pans is alarmingly at variance with the camera's inability to keep still. There follows the staged guerrilla attack and Robin's abduction. Robin's telepathic powers (obliquely alluded to in the conversation with his father) are subsequently revealed to be the cause for the attack, which was used as a diversion to allow Childress to kidnap him.

The notion of hemorrhages--either literal (ruptures of blood vessels) or figurative (manifested as tears in the fabric of placidity built up within the film at various points) becomes THE FURY's governing principle. The opening beach scene is "hemorrhaged" by the guerrilla raid, which culminates in a literal hemorrhage when Peter shoots Childress in the arm. The same applies to Gillian's lunchroom encounter at school, during which her ability to see into a classmate's mind disrupts what began as a pleasant scene (albeit with disturbing undertones, which similarly existed during the Sandza/Childress beach scene) but ends in violence as Gillian's friend is caused to suffer a violent nosebleed.

There follow other powerful demonstrations of Gillian's as-yet-uncontrollable power, which at various times causes the Paragon Institute director, Jack McKeever (Charles Durning)[1] and his assistant to bleed; in the latter's case, profusely. In the meantime, Robin is wreaking havoc of his own. He is being brainwashed by Childress into believing that his father is dead, murdered by the Arab-garbed guerrillas. This mode of dress later triggers Robin to violate the placidity of an amusement park by causing a ferris wheel car with some Arabs in it to spin off its hinges and crash into a restaurant table at which some other Arabs are sitting, a delightful homage to the out-of-control carousel sequence at the end of Hitchcock's STRANGERS ON A TRAIN.

The comparisons between the film's major character doubles adds an appreciable amount of structure to a film that is clearly in love with special effects. Thus, the cool, virtually emotionless Childress (dead like his dead arm: "I killed his arm," Peter boasts), the man whose automaton-like agents are apparently everywhere, dresses always in dark suit and tie. He is contrasted with the moral, independent agent Sandza, who acts spontaneously (but not necessarily recklessly), dresses casually, and is alive to every available opportunity, even making us feel that he is having fun outwitting both the police and Childress' omnipresent henchmen.

Gillian and Robin, the film's psychic doubles, also

Opposite: THE FURY's Childress (John Cassavetes) and Robin (Andrew Stevens) and, above, their counterparts: Gillian (Amy Irving) and Peter (Kirk Douglas). The complementarity of the shots is intentional.

share many qualities. Their powers increase as the film
proceeds, with the distinction that Gillian's power always
seems less controlled than Robin's. Her visions are for
the most part spontaneous, whereas we may infer that at
Childress's hideout, Robin is being trained to channel his
powers as they develop (this is clear from his manipulation
of the ferris wheel car and his self-willed levitations at the
film's end). And, just as Childress and Sandza are aware,
almost psychically, of each other's presence ("I know he's
out there," Childress says at one point), so too does Robin
realize that he is being pursued by the psychically-guided
Gillian who, along with Sandza, is traveling towards Robin
to try to effect his escape.

        The final pairing in the film is again one of compari-
son and contrast. Each agent, the good one and the bad one,
is involved with an attractive woman: Peter with Hester,
Childress with Dr. Susan Charles. Yet the differences between the two relationships are striking. Hester's relationship with Peter is based on mutual affection; Childress and
Susan are clearly only "in business" together. Although both
Hester and Susan have dealings with a psychic youngster, each
uses this involvement for completely opposite reasons: Hester to free Gillian from entrapment at the Paragon Institute,
Susan to use her sexuality as a power (as in CARRIE) to keep
Robin mollified. Hester's sexuality is seen as a healing, re-
demptive force (thus the brief après-sex love scene between
her and Peter in her van), while Susan's is seen as a wicked
tool, used for her "charge's" enslavement.

        The women's cataclysmic ends are in keeping with
these roles. Both die of hemorrhages, but while Hester dies
trying to save Gillian, Susan dies after a final lie to Robin
(she feigns innocence when questioned about who the evening's
dinner guests are and why they are there). Hester, knocked
down and killed by a car, is thus elevated to heroic status;
while Susan, elevated through levitation by her psychic lover
(who holds her in low esteem), is dispatched in grand blood-
bursting paroxysms that to the audience must seem an appropriate end for a woman who uses her body for her own ag-
grandizement.

        Although it runs just under two hours, THE FURY's
pace, editing, and script are so skillfully intermeshed that
there never seems to be a slack moment in the film. The
special effects that the film employs are quite well-realized.
Gillian's visions at Paragon are played out against a rear-

projection backdrop of what she supposedly is seeing. The manner in which foreground and background interact in these scenes
gives the sequences a sense of dimensionality which successfully conveys the vertiginous sensations that Gillian is no
doubt experiencing.

        Peter's cops and robbers chase in the fog with Child-
ress' agents--a chase replete with speeding cars, gunshots,
and terrifyingly limited vision--is a fine microcosmic representation of Peter's entire pursuit of his son, in which only
the psychic Gillian is present to guide him through the miasma
of deceptions that Childress weaves around himself.

        Even the Mother Nuckells sequence, whose comedy
successfully demonstrates De Palma's continued affection for
low humor, not only relieves the tension of the Chicago chase,
but also provides an excellent example of oppression and degradation that mimics the political power plays in which Peter
and Childress are engaged.[2]

One of THE FURY's welcome comic moments. Policeman
Bob (Dennis Franz, center) is about to lose his new car to
the wild-garbed Peter, who will dispose of it in an appropriately dramatic way.

It is this last aspect of THE FURY, its political attitude, that seems somewhat rudimentary and undeveloped. Childress and Peter are both supposedly engaged in government research of psychics. The suggestion is that the cold war of ideas and minor military skirmishes will eventually be supplanted by wars between extrasensory armies fought on mental battlefields. Robin, corrupted by the authoritarian Childress, thus becomes a prototype of the police state psychic, while Gillian--in league with the independent Sandza-- is democracy's darling.

The deaths of Childress and Peter can also be interpreted politically. Peter, realizing that his son is too corrupted to be redeemed, and that escape from Childress is now impossible, commits suicide in an archetypical "give me liberty or give me death" finish. Childress' blinding and demolition by Gillian, separated in time by his stumbling around the room with his hand raised in a mockery of the fascist salute, is the deserved end of all those who oppress the individual will. Gillian atomizes him, so that his body becomes a part of all things in a mock-democratic echoing of Whitman's "look for me under your bootsoles." Doubtless more could have been made of the insidious political machinations behind these characters, but THE FURY is not interested in topical relevance. Instead, the film chooses to give us character types who themselves are only tools in some sketchy global game.

The fact that just before his death Robin seems to transfer his power intact to Gillian (his eyes take on a curious blue glow which, when he dies, is mirrored in hers) hints at the emergence of a new, totally psychic individual, complete both with comprehensive powers and control of them, but free from political influence (thus Gillian's refusal of Childress' offer to be like a father to her). [3] There is the suggestion that an enlightened use of psychic power may be possible, yet the restraint that enlightenment implies is hardly present in Gillian's dispatching of Childress, whether his fate is deserved or not. First consigning his soul to perdition ("You go to Hell"), she then literally explodes him. And De Palma, so delighted with this final set piece (can he ever hope to top it in any of his films' closures?), shows it to us not once but three times, catering to our desire to see the cinematic trick performed over and over again. At THE FURY's finale, Childress, the childless, cold (chill) man in dark, death-like garb (dress) is totally blown apart. Only his head remains intact, which the impish camera, shooting

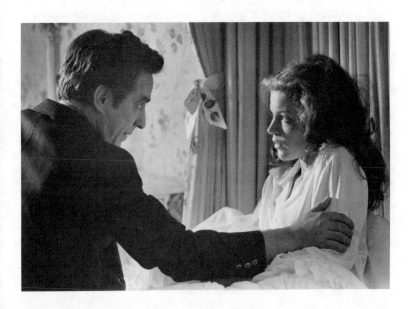

Childress again attempts to control a psychic youngster, Gillian. He is soon to be unpleasantly surprised.

from above in a god's eye shot, shows us rising in typical
De Palma slow motion towards the viewer and then gently
arcing back down to bounce once before De Palma--in a
swift cut to black--shuts the door of this devilish, all-stops-
out binge of a film in our face as though to say, "the show's
over, come back next time." When the spectator does return to De Palma's next full-scale production (DRESSED TO
KILL), it is to the world of PSYCHO, which has been so
corrupted and maliciously transformed that it is virtually
unrecognizable.

NOTES

1.   Durning here reprises the weak authority figure role that
      he perfected in SISTERS.
2.   Peter's entire handling of the Nuckells family, his exag-
      gerated lunacy in front of the two "kidnapped" cops,

and the outrageousness of the disguise he assumes to escape from Childress' henchmen (a disguise featuring toothpaste in the hair for grayness, a pillow stuffed under the shirt for a paunch) are vintage De Palma humor and lovely examples of a comic relief welcome in such a high-tension film.

3. There is a hint of some sexual tension between Gillian and Childress in their last scene together, but it is never developed.

HOME MOVIES is a film that De Palma made with students at Sarah Lawrence College while he was director-in-residence there between 1977 and 1979. It is a lighthearted and free-spirited romp, and to treat it too seriously would be disproportionate. Still, HOME MOVIES does attract interest for the things it shows us about De Palma's directing style and his apparently unquenchable thirst for borrowing from other films, even his own.

The film is openly, one could almost say blatantly, self-reflexive. As its title implies, it's a film about films--movies from home, a movie about home that homes in on movies. Kirk Douglas is The Maestro, director in residence at Now College, who is conducting a course in "Star Therapy" in which students headline in their films and their lives by capturing the latter on film. Already proposed, then, is a strong link between reel and real life. To firm up this connection, even The Maestro's lectures are being filmed; they are, in fact, the movie that HOME MOVIES opens with.

Douglas's brash, intentionally artificial, bigger-than-life manner is wonderfully employed here. When he stops a talkative student from distracting him by planting a severe punch on the student's jaw (after quoting two lines--"I can beat him; you know I can beat him"--that seem lifted from his starring vehicle, CHAMPION), the student attempts to retaliate. Douglas yells, "Great! Cut!" and the adversary is quelled through the invocation of cinematic magic.

We're led into HOME MOVIES' ostensible story (or rather its story within a story) when Douglas has photos of one of his former students, Dennis Byrd (Keith Gordon), flashed on a screen. Dennis is glimpsed sitting forlornly on his suitcase in the middle of a railroad station. He has flunked the star therapy course and become, in The Maestro's words, "an extra in his own life." We then move via flashback to the beginning of Dennis' woeful tale.

Enter the entire Byrd family. Papa Byrd (Vincent Gardenia) is a lecherous doctor. Momma Byrd (Mary Davenport) is the self-consciously suffering type who pretends to swallow sleeping pills when she learns of her husband's latest infidelity (the ruse backfires, though; Papa pumps her stomach anyway). The oldest son, James, is a teacher at the college, lecturing students on what he refers to as "Spartanetics" (a name that recalls SPARTACUS with Douglas as its super-masculine lead character). As played by Gerrit Graham, James is a farcical poseur who blatantly manipulates his as-yet-unbedded fiancée, Christina (Nancy Allen).

James (Gerrit Graham) and his Spartanetics students in HOME MOVIES. The slogan on the T-shirts reveals only half of the course's comically inane slogan: "Those who know ... know."

The gags are fast and numerous in HOME MOVIES.
Most of them arise out of situations involving one or more
of the characters watching (and usually filming) each other.
Dennis believes that his mother has discovered him embrac-
ing a young girl.   Mother spies father dallying with a female
patient.   Christina espies James demonstrating "the proper
mounting of a woman" on one of his Spartanetics disciples
(who have apostle names like Mark, Matthew, and Luke);
while James has his students (replete with cameras and binoculars) spying on Christina, whom he is putting through a
five-level purification rite.   Even Grandma Byrd gets into
the act, sitting at the base of the stairs in the family home
(where she expects the soon-to-be-wed Christina to descend)
with her movie lights and Super-8 camera.

In the meantime, Dennis has been instructed by The
Maestro to film his own life (the results are disastrous)
while The Maestro pops in and out of selected scenes--al-
ways being filmed, and always caught in the glare of a por-
table lighting unit, with a microphone conspicuously dangling
into the frame to catch each of his Hollywoodian phrases.

What we have in HOME MOVIES is various groups
watching the Byrds while the Byrds at the same time watch
(and film) themselves.   What can we conclude but that Byrd-
watching is what defines these various characters' identities;
it is only through being watched that the Byrds and their as-
sociates discover their true selves.

As if all of this Byrd-watching business weren't self-
reflexive enough, De Palma thickens the plot by not only having non-professionals play thinly-disguised versions of themselves (James's students, a campus policeman), but also by
sewing into the film numerous cross references to other films.
I have already mentioned the SPARTACUS and CHAMPION
references.   Others are even more blatant.

In HOME MOVIES' latter half, Christina is run over
by an ambulance.   The shot is composed and presented in
such a way that it becomes a shockingly familiar repetition
of Hester's slow-motion death scene in THE FURY.

The policeman whom Dennis employs to catch his father
in flagrante delicto is an overweight racial bigot who in both
name (Quinn) and size is a slightly reduced version of Orson
Welles' bigoted Hank Quinlan in TOUCH OF EVIL.

It is noteworthy that Keith Gordon (like Nancy Allen, Gerrit Graham, and Kirk Douglas) has to date appeared in more than one De Palma film. Douglas's role in THE FURY as the slightly eccentric Peter Sandza is a more serious version of HOME MOVIES' resourceful Maestro. Gordon's HOME MOVIES character--which is actually revealed to him through a repudiation of The Maestro's film-as-reality dictum (significantly, The Maestro seems to agree with the unreal aspects of film when he tricks Dennis into believing that a film of a woman undressing is real)--is inverted in DRESSED TO KILL, in which he plays a gadget-loving young inventor who successfully spies on Dr. Robert Elliott's office with a Super-8 camera, thus affirming the previously refuted reliance on film as an arbiter of truth.

There is much more in HOME MOVIES that cues the audience into the film's derivative nature, but much of this "business" can be discovered by the viewer himself. Two other points do bear mentioning, though: the derivative theme music by Pino Donaggio, which sounds like a super-pop version of the title music from another school-oriented film, TO SIR WITH LOVE; and the wonderful character of Christina's performing partner, Bunny. This foul-mouthed rabbit (possibly a comically vocal and corrupt descendant of Tommy

HOME MOVIES' Christina (Nancy Allen) and Bunny. Truth from the rabbit hutch. Referring to Christina's sleeping with Dennis, Bunny puts it bluntly: "You fucked him blind, didn't you?"

Smothers' pet in GET TO KNOW YOUR RABBIT) actually
seems to have an existence independent of Christina; that is
if we are to judge by his ability to speak perfectly when
Christina is drugged, and his later-revealed power to speak
without her around at all.   At HOME MOVIES' end, Bunny
carries on the porno-for-fun tradition launched in GREETINGS
and HI, MOM when he is picked up by a young blonde girl
(soon to grow into Carrie?) and asks her, "Wanna be in show
biz, kid?" The humorous interplay between Allen and the
rabbit is quite good, affirming comic talents of the actress
and anticipating the delightful exchanges she has with Detective Marino in DRESSED TO KILL.

In all, HOME MOVIES marks a significant return to
De Palma's relaxed filmmaking techniques, proving that the
anything-for-an-effect, plot-ridden master can still do a successful comic turn when he wants to.

Chapter Eight: TAILORED FOR TERROR

Critics and public alike were somewhat appalled by the blatant reductionism of DRESSED TO KILL, as well as by its
rather harsh treatment of the film's major victim, Kate Miller (Angie Dickinson).   A close examination of the film will
reveal that although it is much more than just a retelling of
PSYCHO, there is ample justification for disparaging its att-
tude toward women.

Like OBSESSION, CARRIE, and THE FURY, DRESSED
TO KILL opens with a lyrical sequence that functionally
serves as a contrast to the violent events to follow.   The
slow-motion camera probes through Kate's bathroom, finally
entering the shower stall along with the woman.   Kate is
seen lathering and caressing herself in a manner reminiscent of Carrie's self-gratification in the shower.   Kate's male
companion (who turns out to be her husband) is in the bathroom with her, but he is oblivious to her actions.   Although
the caresses with which she favors herself could be construed
as substitutes for her husband's advances (she does, after all,
gaze repeatedly in his direction), it turns out that Kate's fantasies are involved solely with imaginary, not real men--in
this case with an unidentified brute who materializes and
crudely assaults her from behind, thrusting his hand between her legs and lifting her off the floor.

There follows a bed scene between Kate and her husband.   After reaching climax, Mr. Miller perfunctorily kisses
his wife on the cheek and then rolls off her.   A brief scene

Kate Miller's (Angie Dickinson) shower fantasy from DRESSED TO KILL, a dream soon to be realized.

between Kate and her inventor son, Peter (Keith Gordon), follows.   Kate then leaves for her appointment with psychiatrist Robert Elliott (Michael Caine).   Judging by their discussion--the main subject is Kate's complaint about her husband's "wham-bam special" and her need for sexual fulfillment (after the doctor agrees with her that she is an attractive woman, she asks why he hasn't propositioned her)--Elliott is probably treating Kate for sexual anxiety.

The film's following events can be quickly summarized. Kate is picked up and seduced by a man she pursues in a museum.   She flees his apartment when she discovers after sex that he has a venereal disease, is attacked and killed in the building's elevator by what appears to be a razor-wielding female.   Her son and a witness to the killing (prostitute Liz Blake, played by Nancy Allen) finally determine that the real killer is Elliott in drag.

Comparisons of DRESSED TO KILL with PSYCHO reveal DRESSED TO KILL's appropriation and modification of the Hitchcock film's universe.   Both films disparage the re-

lationship between sex and money.   The sexual interaction
between Sam Loomis and Marion Crane is crippled by Sam's
alimony payments and Marion's apparently low-paying job.
DRESSED TO KILL's Liz Blake is clearly in the business
of trading her favors for cash, an attitude implicitly criticized, while Kate Miller's upper middle class income provides her with the leisure time to apparently do nothing
more than flirt with her psychiatrist and dawdle in places
like museums.

PSYCHO and DRESSED TO KILL each feature a female protagonist who is killed off early in the production.
In both films, the male killer performs his murders while
attired as a woman.   Norman Bates' and Robert Elliott's
homicidal impulses are linked with sexual desire, with the
distinction that Norman kills detective Arbogast and attempts
to kill Sam Loomis and Lila Crane to avoid capture, whereas
no such self-protective behavior is evidenced by Doctor Elliott's alter ego, Bobby.

PSYCHO's shower scene murder draws much of its

Doctor Elliott (Michael Caine) and Kate Miller (Angie Dickinson) in DRESSED TO KILL.

force from its commission in an enclosed, virtually claustro-
phobic space, one that is normally construed as being safe.
The elevator in DRESSED TO KILL mirrors these conditions
somewhat (elevators are not always considered safe, as indicated by the reflecting mirrors--now standard equipment in
them--to prevent unforeseen assaults). Finally, both films'
murderers are revealed thanks to the efforts of a clue-hunting
male/female pair: Sam and Lila in PSYCHO, Peter and Liz
in DRESSED TO KILL. [1]

There are major differences between the films, however, that demonstrate not only DRESSED TO KILL's unique-
ness, but its essential nastiness as well. Hitchcock somewhat unfairly stacks the deck against Marion Crane before
her murder: not only is she carrying on what she herself
regards as an illicit love affair ("Sam this is the last time
... for meeting you in secret ... we can even have dinner,
but respectably," says Marion) but she is also a thief, a woman
who steals $40,000 from an employer who has trusted her
for over ten years.

DRESSED TO KILL also is biased against its victim,
Kate Miller, but in a curious way (and herein may be seen
the source for the objections raised against the film by so
many viewers). The film's opening scenes give us a picture
of Kate as a woman with sado-masochistic sexual tendencies.
Her need for degradation as a prelude to sexual satisfaction
is demonstrated in the only gratifying sexual encounter for her
the film portrays: with the driver watching the entire scene,
she is masturbated in a taxicab by the man she has met in
the museum. The scene's voyeuristic elements suggest that
an appreciable degree of Kate's pleasure here derives from
being watched. (This characteristic establishes an implicit
similarity between Kate and Elliott, since the latter's repeated
glances into a framed mirror on his desk for self-assurance
smacks of pleasure derived from self-observance.)

Kate's promiscuity is portrayed as the direct cause of
her undoing. Had she not made a pass at Elliott, and then
dallied with the man in the museum, she would not have been
murdered. Moreover, the cruel twist of the venereal disease
report indicates that in the film's cosmos, either disease or
death (or both) are the inevitable outcomes of indiscriminate
sexuality. True, Liz's promiscuity helps to solve the case,
but at a tremendous cost. As her nightmare dream at the
film's end reveals, she has been permanently scarred by her
encounter with Elliott.

There is also something insidiously premeditated about
the use of Angie Dickinson for the part of Kate Miller. Where
Janet Leigh in PSYCHO radiated a healthy naturalness in her
early talk with a fellow employee and, later, with Norman in
his parlor, Dickinson projects annoyingly studied, one might
almost say affected, character traits. Unlike Leigh, who
literally lets her hair down in PSYCHO's shower scene,
Dickinson remains immaculately coiffed throughout the bathing, never getting even a single strand of her hair wet. Her
faked responses in bed (as opposed to what we may assume
to be Leigh's unstudied reactions with Sam) are, while regrettable, annoying as well, a type of dissembling that seems
to fit in with her role as a pampered woman (the sleek apartment,
the expensive clothes, the lavish ring she wears), idle, promiscuous, concerned with appearances and more interested
in compiling a grocery list in the museum (a list scribbled
with a gold-plated pen) than in looking at the pieces of art.
A friend of mine once noted that Dickinson looks like a high-
priced whore; one has to admit the remark's truthfulness.
Although her hands belie traces of age (the shots of her body
in the shower are those of a stand-in), her face is miraculously line-free, doubtless the result of time and money spent
on elaborate skin preparations. The combination of the traits
of Dickinson-the-actress (which I suspect made her in De
Palma's view such an apt choice for the part of Kate Miller)
and the attributes of the character herself, give us what appears to be a picture of a cheap, promiscuous woman.

I use the words "cheap" and "promiscuous" here because it is the attitude that DRESSED TO KILL takes towards
both Kate in particular and sexual activity in general. We
are prevented from seeing Kate's involvement with the man
in the museum as anything but a lustful act that merits retribution. Even if we try to view Kate's behavior as merely
that of a love-starved woman dying for release, we are nevertheless biased against this view by the inclusion of the venereal disease report, which not only makes the whole afternoon's (unseen) dalliance seem rather sordid, but also reflects the director's attitude towards her, an attitude that
allows De Palma to play the very nasty trick on Kate of
virtually upbraiding her for her actions. This judgmental
approach to sex, only playfully proposed in PSYCHO as an
ironic undercurrent to the film's action (keyed by the change
in color of Marion's underwear from the early white she
wears during her idyll with Sam, which ends in her vowing
never to meet him again under similar conditions, to the
black she wears after the robbery), is presented seriously

in DRESSED TO KILL. Given Kate's fantasy about being attacked in the shower, her murder can be viewed as merely
the fulfillment of her desire for brutalization.

In fact, sexual fulfillment within a traditional heterosexual relationship is seen as virtually impossible in the film.
Liz is a prostitute; Dr. Elliott is a disturbed man in the
midst of having a sex-change operation (it is interesting to
speculate whether he would have been capable of heterosexual
sex if his operation had been completed); Kate's husband fails
to satisfy her, while the innocent and promising relationship
between Liz and Peter is, within the film, never consummated.

Instead, in a reprise of CARRIE's ending, we are
shown Liz's nightmare about Dr. Elliott's escaping from the
psychiatric ward, dressing as a nurse, slipping into Kate's
bathroom, and slitting Liz's throat--a fantasy that strongly
mirrors Kate's bathroom musings right down to the attack
from the rear, thereby suggesting that both women view themselves as sexual victims: Kate at the hands of her husband,
Liz at the hands of men like Elliott who try to take advantage
of her. It is reasonable to extrapolate from this similarity
that Liz's experience with Dr. Elliott has somehow suggested
to her how strongly most sexual relationships are characterized by power plays, and how her role as a prostitute
necessarily puts her in the position of the victimized sexual
item that men purchase for their pleasure. Like Kate with
her wealthy husband, Liz has repeatedly sold herself for
money. (There is a hint, however, that the relationship
with Peter may change this situation.)

Nevertheless, within the film's action, sexuality is
portrayed as either vulgar, debased, or alienating. Liz was
not, as she claims in the police station, visiting a friend at
the apartment building where Kate was murdered. Detective
Marino (Dennis Franz) puts it bluntly, "Who were you fuck-
ing?" The profanity is used intentionally to awaken us to the
distinction between a romantic liaison (an example of which
DRESSED TO KILL gives us none) and a business meeting.

In the place of normal sex, DRESSED TO KILL offers
us degradation and inversion. Dr. Robert Elliott's character
brings out this aspect of the film most clearly. When Kate
propositions him, Elliott glances into a picture frame on his
desk that contains a mirror. He repeats this action when
Liz strips down to Fredericks of Hollywood brassiere and
panties to distract him. The mirror suggests that what ex-

Liz (Nancy Allen) and DRESSED TO KILL's murderous blonde
during the elevator sequence.

cites Elliott about women who make advances to him is not
the idea of going to bed with them but the idea of this hap-
pening to <u>him</u>, the handsome devil he sees in the mirror.
And when he compulsively changes into his female attire to
consummate the act with a razor instead of a penis (becoming in both dress and actions a complementary character to
SISTERS' Dominique), it is as though his female alter ego,
Bobby, was gaining satisfaction from his male side, the side
that these women are attracted to, the side that the woman-
ish Bobby will soon have all to him (her?) self. [2]

        With his pending operation, Elliott is on the verge of
being a perfect, self-contained, independent sexual unit, com-
bining the aggressive and passive sexual roles in one person.
The twist is that the usual sexual associations with these
modes of behavior are reversed in him. It is Elliott's female side, the side with the castrating razor, that is the
sexual aggressor, while the male side is passive. The slay-

ing of Kate by Bobby[3] can also be viewed as an expression
of Elliott's alarm and disgust with his male personality, the
side that attracts women. The razor solves Elliott's problem
in two ways; first by slaying the temptress, and later--in the
guise of the surgical scalpel to be used in the sex-change op-
eration--by eliminating the most obvious symbol of Elliott's
masculinity: his penis.

Elliott teaches aggressive women who want to seduce
his male side a grievous lesson by inducing in them the ultimate passivity--death--and by leaving only the barest, mock-
ing traces of sexuality behind, as in the convulsive contrac-
tions of Kate's hand as she writhes on the elevator floor in
the last orgasmic throes of death. The element of sexual
disgust, present in PSYCHO and SISTERS, and first presented
here in the venereal disease report, reaches full fruition in
the explicit discussion about sex-change surgical procedures
between Liz and Peter in a restaurant, a conversation that
(somewhat comically) turns a fellow patron (Mary Davenport)
quite nauseous.

There is no doubt that DRESSED TO KILL is the most
polished and assured De Palma film to date. Caine and Dickinson lend star value to the by-now-familiar theatrics of suspense, while Allen--reprising the role of the little sexpot she
perfected in CARRIE--acts this time on the side of the law
and demonstrates a genuine flair for comedy (especially in her
scenes with Marino).

DRESSED TO KILL's finale is clearly a CARRIE-like
ending, complete with back-from-the-grave threat (Elliott at
this point is presumably interred in a mental ward) and slow
motion photography, a device that, as in CARRIE, should warn
the viewer that a reprise of the present film's opening dis-
turbance is about to occur.[4] Yet the manner in which Liz's
dream is presented is so engaging that by its very strange-
ness and exaggeration we can almost take it to be real. The
murder of the nurse in the mental ward, and Elliott's slow
walk to Peter's house to find Liz in the bathroom, have the
force of a bad dream coming true. After all, if your closest
confidante, a psychiatrist, can betray your confessions by
murdering you, then anything is possible.

The film's end may not have the terror value of CAR-
RIE's pseudo-resurrection, but the shock of seeing Elliott in
slow motion draw a straight razor blade across Liz's neck is
sufficient. DRESSED TO KILL ends with Peter comforting the

terrorized Liz in a fashion identical to Sue Snell's mother's comforting of her frightened young daughter, right down to the position that the characters assume.

Filmgoers who found DRESSED TO KILL objectionable because of its jaundiced view of sexuality and its unfair treatment of its female characters have cause for speaking out. The film is offensive: sex, particularly female sexuality, is presented as something loathsome. The fact that De Palma is having fun with the proceedings (and making money as well; DRESSED TO KILL is the highest-grossing De Palma film to date) only makes matters worse. Hitchcock did virtually the same thing with repulsion and sexuality seventeen years earlier, yet the differences between the films' approaches and treatments are painfully obvious. There is a black humor to PSYCHO that doesn't operate in DRESSED TO KILL. As a consequence, the latter film appears to be exploiting violence. Were this not the case, and had De Palma leavened the film with a bit more of the puckish humor that he so successfully used previously, DRESSED TO KILL might have been one of his greatest aesthetic successes instead of merely his biggest money-maker.

NOTES

1. A further Hitchcock cross-reference can be seen in Elliott's female garb, which virtually duplicates the disguise worn by Karen Black in FAMILY PLOT.
2. Two other examples of Elliott's narcissism, his love affair with himself, should be noted. Listening to Bobby's message on his telephone answering machine, Elliott hears Bobby rhetorically ask, who is committing the murders? Immediately thereafter, Elliott glances into a mirror, thus providing us with an answer. Later, when Liz plays seducer with Elliott, she asks, "I find you sexually attractive; what about you?" The sentence's elliptical question ("how do you feel about me?" is only implied) makes Elliott's affirmative reply seem to refer less to Liz's appeal than to his attraction to himself, as though he were saying, "Yes, I find me sexually attractive," which--given the film's mirror references--we can see to be quite true.
3. The character's name is an obvious and unfortunate tip-off to the murderer's identity. Although this information is withheld long enough to create some suspense, it is quite plain when Elliott goes looking for Bobby

at a hospital that he is really looking for himself. In
DRESSED TO KILL's last half, we know who the murderer is. De Palma should have kept PSYCHO in
mind at this point; the Hitchcock film only reveals
the murderer's real identity at the end, and even
then--with the film's final twist arising out of Mrs.
Bates' last soliloquy--we are not totally sure who
really committed the crimes.

4.   Key elements in the DRESSED TO KILL scene make this
section a virtual duplication of the earlier film's ending. Carrie attacks Sue with her right hand while the
latter is bending over the grave; Elliott grabs the
nurse who is bending over his "grave" (the hospital
bed where, as a functionally and supposedly "dead"
character, he is buried) with his right hand. Similarly, the match cut at CARRIE's end is duplicated
in DRESSED TO KILL as Liz, waking from her dream,
is comforted by Peter (who, like Mrs. Snell, approaches from the left) to no avail. The fact that
during and immediately after Elliott's attack Pino
Donaggio employs music almost identical to that used
at CARRIE's comparable point only strengthens the
indebtedness of this portion of DRESSED TO KILL to
its predecessor.

With BLOW OUT, De Palma returns to the political concerns
obliquely dealt with in THE FURY, employs the cinematic devices of suspense made use of in virtually all of his films,
and combines these qualities with a flair for storytelling and
a gift for visual expression unequalled in any of his other
work. Apparently, De Palma has reached the point in his
career at which he does not have to strain for effects (as
he was accused of doing in THE FURY). Having jettisoned
the extremely objectionable attitudes towards sexuality which
were exhibited in DRESSED TO KILL, and taken as his subject a political assassination that draws upon the John Kennedy
killing, Watergate,[1] and Chappaquiddick, De Palma manages
to produce a film that is both entertaining and politically ap-
posite. In addition, he demonstrates within the film a command of parallel action and symbolic framing that has rarely
seemed more assured.

BLOW OUT begins with a typical De Palma device:
the film (or, as in the case of SISTERS, the television show)
within a film, as though the director wished constantly to remind us how automatically (and often incorrectly) we assign
verisimilitude to what we see.

The tracking camera takes the point of view of a stalk-
ing killer. In HALLOWEEN style, we creep up on a girl's
dormitory, where a policeman/voyeur is gazing through a
window at two scantily-dressed dancing coeds. A knife is
raised and the policeman falls. Eventually, the killer (who,

like Robert Montgomery in LADY IN THE LAKE, is revealed in a mirror) stalks into a steamy bathroom (much like the one in DRESSED TO KILL's opening and close), draws back the shower curtain à la PSYCHO, and raises his knife.   The young woman in the shower screams (actually, whines is a better word for the embarrassing sound that emerges from her), and De Palma cuts to show us that what we are watching is the workprint of the latest Independence Pictures Incorporated production (Coed Frenzy) that soundman Jack Terri (John Travolta) is working on.

The head of Independence Films tells Jack that they need to replace some of the film's sound effects, in particular the scream and the wind sounds.   Jack's boss will supply the "screamers"; Jack must get a new recording of howling wind.

This sequence of events brings Jack to a bridge late at night, a bridge off which the car of Presidential candidate Governor George McRyan plunges.   Jack, seeing the crash, dives down into the water, notes that the car's male occupant is dead, and rescues the other passenger, Sally Bedina (Nancy

BLOW OUT's soundman, Jack Terri (John Travolta), soon to become embroiled in a corrupt, convoluted plot.

Allen). Back at the hospital, Jack discovers the identity of
the dead man and agrees to the Governor's aide's request
that he completely forget the whole incident.

The snag is that Jack, as a soundman, has recorded
the accident and is biased in favor of the apparently objective
evidence on his recorder, which indicates that the Governor,
instead of sustaining a flat, had his tire shot out by someone
wielding a rifle.

The case begins to resemble an amalgamation of Watergate, Chappaquiddick, and Dallas on November 23, 1963. A
call to Presidential Campaign Manager Jack Matters from a
man named Burke (John Lithgow) reveals that Burke took it
upon himself to cause the accident, not knowing (or so he
claims) that the governor would be killed. [2] Burke's language,
full of usages like "objective achieved," "parameters of error," and "completely secure our operation," combined with
his unprincipled, gung-ho ideas about the ruination of the in-
cumbent President's potential opponents, brands him as a true
G. Gordon Liddy type. Additionally, the plunge into the water of a car carrying a Presidential hopeful and a young girl
bears too close a resemblance to the Teddy Kennedy Chappaquiddick incident to be coincidental. (The difference between
Chappaquiddick and this event in BLOW OUT is that here it
is the politician who gets killed, not the [presumably] innocent young woman.) The John Kennedy assassination is
present when Burke, attempting to erase all evidence of his
crime, stops by a garage where McRyan's car is stored to
replace the blown-out tire and for a moment bends down to
finger the entrance and exit holes in the tire left by the bul-
let he fired--a painful reminder of the obsession with entrance and exit wounds that became such a vital part of the
Warren Commission testimony and inquiry. Finally, the
Kennedy assassination emerges once again in the person of
Manny Karp (a fishy man with a fishy name, played by Dennis Franz) who happens to have filmed the entire crash.
Jack purchases copies of the news magazine featuring frame
enlargements from Karp's film and syncs the pictures to his
soundtrack of the event. The result is that he now has a
totally faithful record of the incident, one with both sound
and image.

Unfortunately, the police are not interested in Jack's
evidence. Detective Mackey informs Jack that "a special
commission will find that it [the Governor's death] was an
accident." [3] In this <u>Alice in Wonderland</u> universe, the ver-

dict comes before the trial, a situation that many critics of
the Warren Commission charged was in operation during the
Commission's ostensible investigation.

Yet the media are interested--in particular Frank Donohue, a reporter for a local Philadelphia television station.[4]
Donohue suggests that Jack and Sally appear on his news show
to present their evidence. Unfortunately, the phone calls
made to arrange this appearance are being tapped by Burke
(whom we have seen twice posing as a Bell System repair-
man. Thus both Watergate and McRyan-gate have their respective utility company operatives: the former has "the
plumbers"; the latter, "the phone man"). Burke, posing as
Donohue, waylays Sally, and eventually, while being pursued
by Jack, garrotes her with a wire that runs out of a special
compartment in his wristwatch. Jack arrives too late to
save Sally, although in time to prevent Burke from tattooing
an image of the Liberty Bell on Sally's chest with an icepick,
a diversionary tactic he had used on a previous victim whom
he mistook for Sally, and which thus leads the newspapers to
speak of a "Liberty Bell murderer."[5] Jack then kills the
agent with his own weapon.

From its opening credits, BLOW OUT establishes a
tone of assured artistry and maintains it throughout the production. The sounds that accompany the names of the film's
three most important participants are extraordinarily apt,
cluing us into the need to pay attention to the simultaneity
of sound and image (and, as we shall see, sometimes image
and image) within the film. When De Palma's name appears,
we hear heavy breathing, suggesting the leering noises made
by a voyeur (the director as the ultimate Peeping Tom), as
well as an anticipation of the heavy breathing in the audience
that this latest cinematic effort will occasion. (The fact that
this heavy breathing is revealed to be that of Coed Frenzy's
murderer also implies that De Palma and he are somehow
related; and in a sense they are, in that, ultimately, the
director is the man responsible for all of BLOW OUT's kill-
ings.)

Travolta's name appears, and we hear the high-pitched
whine of a recording device, an appropriate effect for the
character of a sound technician, especially one whose virtually obsessive bias in favor of aural evidence causes the
deaths of two innocent people: Freddy, a policeman who
was acting as an undercover agent on an investigation of police corruption (the King Commission), and Sally who--like
the policeman--is wired for sound by Jack.

Finally, when Nancy Allen's name appears, we hear
a scream--totally apt for her character, who becomes the
victim of Burke's homicidal tendencies and whose scream
for help at BLOW OUT's end is, somewhat cruelly, given
immortality in Independence Pictures' latest film.

Although within BLOW OUT's story there are denials,
dead ends, murdered witnesses, and finally (we may reasonably assume) a complete abandonment of the pursuit of the
conspiracy theory by Jack (who will doubtless retreat back
into harmless inaction after trying for a second time to do
some good, with the same result as before: someone's
death),[6] the film is inundated with visual and verbal clues
that tell the audience what is going to happen, and to whom.
Two cinematic devices communicate the sense of ironic fatality that hangs over the film: simultaneity and verbal foreshadowing.

There are two kinds of simultaneity in BLOW OUT:
temporal and physical. By temporal simultaneity I mean
that two actions occurring at the same time are either represented purely simultaneously (within the same frame) or
through parallel editing, these actions thus becoming implicitly
linked in the audience's minds--although the characters always miss these coincidences. (De Palma uses his formerly
favorite device for simultaneity, the split screen, once in
BLOW OUT, in a telephone conversation between Jack and
Sally, and here the device seems more like a parody of a
1930s slashed-screen effect then a resurrection of the technique's former meaningful uses.)

On the telephone with Sally after speaking with Donohue, Jack fails to hear a siren howling in the background,
which we can justifiably assume (given Burke's recent dis-
closure of the body's whereabouts to the police) is that of an
ambulance going to pick up the body of Mary Robert, whom
Burke has mistaken for Sally. The connection between the
sound outside (the siren, in response to a murder) and the
woman on the phone (soon to be murdered by Burke) naturally
completely eludes Jack. Additionally, the siren has the effect of causing Jack to miss hearing what Sally tells him at
this moment ("I never watch the news"), thus ensuring that
Jack will allow her to meet Burke (posing as Donohue) alone
and thereby virtually guaranteeing her demise.

Burke, pretending to be Donohue, calls Sally at home,
while at the same time Jack fails to pay attention to the tele-

vision show that discusses Mary's death.   Again, because
Jack is unaware of everything that is going on in the McRyan
case, he is unable to draw any connection between the death
of this young woman and the existence of his female friend.
The implications here are fairly shocking: while Jack pursues his own investigation, which he thinks will lead him to
the real truth about McRyan's death, there is, unbeknownst
to him, a further layer of truth--a more insidious, repellent
truth--at work underneath everything, a truth that only De
Palma and the audience share.   (Even after Jack kills Burke,
he still does not know that the dead man is the one responsible for McRyan's death.)

     In another scene, Burke is on the phone telling Mat-
ters that he will clean up his operation's loose ends by "ter-
minating" the girl.   At the same time, Jack is in the sound
studio dubbing in screams, an action he will--thanks to Burke
--finally bring to a successful conclusion when he dubs Sally's
recorded calls for help (during Burke's attempt to kill her)
into the film he is working on.

     BLOW OUT also employs physical simultaneity--the
symbolic placing within the frame of people and objects that
represent important clues (or hints about clues) about Mc-
Ryan's death and Burke's actions--to establish ironic linkages
for us.   During one of BLOW OUT's early scenes, Jack,
prior to going out on location, is working in his studio dubbing sounds and listening to various recordings.   Jack is in
the rear of the frame while nearer the camera a television
drones on about Governor McRyan's trip to the Liberty Ball,
a trip that will be cut short by his accident.   At this point
in the film, Jack is still in the background of the story:
thus his symbolic position in the frame while, although
neither Jack nor the audience yet knows it, the Governor
and his soon-to-occur accident are coming into the action's
foreground, a movement suggested by the television's placement within the scene.

     Outside, on the bridge, Jack is seen in the background
in deep focus, with an owl (and later a frog) in the foreground.   These two harmless animals are then joined by an
unseen third animal whose sound (resembling that of a cricket
or cicada) is picked up by Jack's microphone.   Then, as with
the shots of the owl and the frog, we get a shot from the
vantage point of this third animal, a higher order beast that
turns out to be Burke, who is playing with his self-styled
garrote.   That Burke--like the Governor in death--is soon

to come into prominence in BLOW OUT is suggested not only
by his placement in the frame's foreground and the mysteri-
ous nature of the sound that he makes, but also by the attribute that elevates him over the two previously glimpsed crea-
tures: his ability to be invisible.

A virtual parallel of the animal scene is achieved in
the sequence within which Burke spots Sally (it is actually
Mary Robert) in a department store. Burke, the unseen animal, is now visible, but his symbolic placement within the
frame is the same as before. Standing impressively in the
foreground and holding a photo of Sally, who he thinks is
descending an escalator, Burke looks down on his victim
while the young woman, further away from the camera, appears small and helpless as she moves down out of the frame
into nothingness.

Tailing Mary in an arcade, Burke is followed by the
tracking camera. A young man carrying a bloody slab of
beef passes Burke. As if this hint at butchery were not
foreshadowing enough, we get three further clues about the
fate of Burke's prey. The camera stops tracking at a food
counter. In the foreground, on ice, is a dead fish lying on
its side. Next to it is an icepick, which Burke steals (he
will use this instrument on both Mary and Sally). The pick
is obviously the murder weapon, soon to be put to use, while
the connotations of the ice ("to ice" colloquially means "to
kill" while "being on ice" equals death) and the dead fish are
quite obvious. Again, a suggestion of butchery appears, this
time in the persons of two men just beyond the fish counter
who are standing over large pieces of raw meat.

In the scene during which Jack worked while the de-
tails of McRyan's itinerary were reported on television, Jack
was engaged in re-recording sounds labeled "Gunshot," "Wind,"
"Body Fall," and "Glass Breaks" (effects that can be seen to
apply to McRyan's forthcoming accident). De Palma here in-
troduces another framing device by breaking up the image into
various planes. In the present scene, it is a partition to the
immediate left of the television that divides Jack from the
important information being imparted on television; he could
not possibly recognize the significance of the information;
thus the barrier of ignorance connoted by the "wall" between
him and the television receiver.

In the arcade sequence with Burke and Mary, the metal
retainer at the end of the glass food case breaks the image

into two planes of focus, suggesting a disparity among all of
the scenes's elements that may yet, somehow, be resolved.
Contending with this sense of divisiveness is the fact that
within this scene, the fish, the ice, the meat, Burke, and
Mary are all seen in focus, suggesting a relationship among
them.   One finds in BLOW OUT that it is only after Mary's
murder that these opposing forces are resolved; until then,
the scene's many elements, although joined in terms of focus, threaten to break apart in terms of the way they are
arranged within the frame. 7

Jack is again linked with information that for the moment fails to help him in his quest when he loses Sally in the
railroad station.   Alternatively posed beneath signs for the
"Franklin Bridge Express" and the "Upper Level, " he im-
potently stands there waiting for an aural clue from Sally as
to her whereabouts.

In all of these scenes, De Palma is careful to have
the action occur in such a way that foreground and background information are never perceived as linked by the film's characters, suggesting that BLOW OUT's view of the prospects
for truth, within politics in particular and the world in general, is extremely pessimistic.

Further, as De Palma implies, all of our electronics,
our sophisticated information-gathering machines, fail to bring
us any closer to the facts in a particular situation.   Neither
Jack's recording nor the Karp film can begin to account for
the web of misalliances, conflicting desires, cross-purposes
and shady deals that seem to lie just in back of any attempt
to illegally affect the electoral process.   We may presume
that there is even more to BLOW OUT's conspiracy than we
see.   What will Karp's fate be?   (Curiously, we never see
Burke attempting to find Karp and destroy his evidence.)
Was Burke a lone aberrant, as Matters suggests, or was he
rather quite representative of the devoted hangers-on that any
candidate garners?   How much are we to believe of John
Mitchell look-alike Matters' claim that Burke has gone too
far?   Matters' disavowal of Burke's operation ("What operation?" he asks the agent) seems somewhat suspect, since he
must, at least unconsciously, have known about Burke's re-
liability and values before he engaged him.   And after all,
Burke has effectively eliminated McRyan, who will never (like
Teddy Kennedy) be able to even attempt a political resurrection.

        Jack, the self-confessed gadget-loving kid-turned-
soundman, inadvertently sabotages a police department investigation of corruption within the ranks because he forgets
that Freddy, the man he "wired," might sweat and thereby
corrode the battery strapped to him.[8] Jack seems to overlook the fact that people get nervous in tense situations, an
attitude consistent with a young man whose total trust (until
BLOW OUT's end) is in "cool" electronics (photography, tape
recording), rather than difficult, "warm" human emotions,
to reveal the truth. Jack allows Sally to walk into a trap
with the supposed Frank Donohue (even though Donohue never
called him back as agreed, which should have indicated to
Jack a suspicious irregularity) because he places his faith
in the "wire" he attaches to the young woman. Despite his
electronics' aid in helping him locate the scene of Sally's assault, they are not sufficient to guarantee Jack's arrival there
in time to save the girl. Interestingly, though, Jack sits up
in the ambulance when Sally asks Burke, whom she still at
this point believes to be Donohue: "Why are you wrapping it
up?" (The phrase relates to Burke's tying up the film Sally
has brought him with Jack's tape, although the words also
suggest that Burke is finally tying up the case's loose ends
as he moves closer to his murder of the girl.) Jack's reaction, which occurs before he plugs his earphone back in,
suggests that he is, at this late juncture, beginning to ac-
quire the ability to react humanly (or, in this case, extra-
humanly) to people in distress, instead of merely electronically, like a machine. Nevertheless, by BLOW OUT's finale,
Jack returns to the cool responses consistent with an equipment addict, never again (apparently) to trust his human sen-
sitivity which, in any case, manifests itself too late to save
Sally.

        The character of Jack bears comparison with the per-
son of De Palma. Both are gadget-lovers; both work with
film and sound; both are investigators of murder, the former
in pursuit of "justice," the latter merely creating suspense
out of homicide for the purpose of providing entertainment.
It is the differences between Jack and De Palma, though, that
are most interesting. Jack thinks he can penetrate to the
truth beneath the actions and statements of the film's characters. For Jack, the truth is ultimately the most important
thing, not the feelings of McRyan's wife ("How would his wife
feel knowing that he died with his hand under some girl's
dress?" McRyan's aide asks, and Jack replies, "It's the
truth, isn't it?") nor the need to resist possibly premature
charges of conspiracy (a reaction of which Mackey accuses
Jack).

De Palma, like Jack, also wants to publish his version of the truth, although his view is that the real facts in
virtually any situation are ultimately unknowable; as such, we
exist in a rather disorderly universe, one in which change
and deception play larger parts than the supposedly fated triumph of good over evil.

If anything, De Palma's insistence throughout BLOW
OUT (and all of his other films as well) on a morbid--albeit
sometimes playfully offered--sense of fatality should indicate
how deeply committed he is to the view of a world within
which terrible things are not only bound to happen, but where
we are usually powerless to do little except observe the oc-
currence of these events.

More so than any of De Palma's other films, BLOW
OUT is filled with ironic and/or fateful dialogue that bleakly
foreshadows the awful events to come. Verbal and visual
foreshadowing meet in the scene between Donohue and Jack
at Independence Pictures' studio. The two men agree that
"someone shot out the tire of McRyan's car," but neither
can determine who it was. De Palma then allows the visu-
als to provide the answer: as a movie poster on the wall
behind Jack and Donohue intimates, it was "The Boogey Man"
who did it. This boogey man allusion refers to more than
just the ethereal presence of Burke, who roams around the
city as a virtually invisible (as in his first "appearance"
near the bridge) entity. (Burke pulls Mary Robert out of a
bus queue in broad daylight while people are boarding the
bus right in front of her.) Recalling BLOW OUT's HALLO-
WEEN-style opening, and the latter film's identification of
its killer as the boogey man, the archetypical image of evil,
we can conclude that what De Palma is here suggesting is
that the man who was responsible for McRyan's death (and
ultimately the deaths of Mary and Sally) is not an individual
so much as a representative of an all-pervasive and peren-
nial evil. Burke, as I suggested earlier, would then be seen
as only one man among the many obsessive individuals in politics, overly devoted agents who would murder for any political reason.

One of BLOW OUT's most fateful foreshadowings is a
purely visual one. McRyan's aide has given Sally a sum of
money to leave town for a few weeks; she and Jack meet at
a train station (with the result that Jack persuades Sally to
remain in town). Talking to Sally at the gate to her train,
Jack stands under a sign giving the train's name as "Cru-
sader," while above Sally a train sign reads "Wall Street."

These train names are very apt designations for the two
characters' respective fates. Jack, we soon realize, is on
a crusade, one might say a virtually religious one, during
which he sacrifices everything (including Sally) to the attain-
ment of the grail of truth. Sally's sign has a more deadly
accuracy, since it is by a wall high over the street that she
is finally garroted and killed by Burke in one of BLOW OUT's
final scenes.

Interviewed on television, Manny Karp states that he
was at the bridge trying out some new film stock that was
"good for night shooting. I do a lot of work at night." The
pun on shooting--referring both to photography and to Mc-
Ryan's murder--is typical of De Palma, as is Karp's ambiguous comment about working at night given his later-revealed
business of blackmailing men by taking photos of them in
evening rendezvous with women (Sally among them) whom he
has hired to play up to the men. Interestingly, one of Karp's
blackmail photos, which is shown to Jack by the policeman
guarding Karp's office, is of Sally and a man in bed in a
motel that, if we are to judge by the wallpaper (red, white,
and blue to match the Liberty Day festivities, and identical
to the colors of Burke's tie as well, thus establishing a tonal
link between him and Sally that will be completed with Sally's
murder), is the same motel in which Sally innocently spends
the night with Jack. The duplication of the wallpaper is such
a small detail that it might be missed unless one were prepared for the barrage of minute clues that De Palma includes
in BLOW OUT. Their profusion suggests further, virtually
unrealizable, conspiracies beyond the ones uncovered in the
film.

In a pre-murder television interview, Presidential Campaign manager Jack Matters (the man who doesn't want to know
about the matters that Burke brings to his attention, but who
nevertheless becomes involved in the matters that another
Jack--Terri--is revealing through his inquiries) talks about
McRyan's impressive showing in the polls. As he points out,
however, "a lot can happen between then [election day] and
now," a statement that acts as an ironic foreshadowing of
McRyan's death as well as a possible admission of the undercover "operation" whose reality Matters denies when speaking
with Burke.

A television commentator on the same show talks about
Governor McRyan's intention to use the Liberty Ball to "throw
his hat into the ring." If we take the word "ball" in the col-

loquial sense of meaning sexual contact, and Sally as Mc-
Ryan's Liberty Ball "ball," then we can take the rest of the
statement to mean that as a result of his involvement with
Sally, McRyan has--inadvertently--thrown his body into the
river instead of his hat into the ring.   The former deadly
action nonetheless results in McRyan's achieving a notoriety
in death possibly equal to the prominence he might have gar-
nered in life had he been elected president.

          In one of BLOW OUT's later scenes, Burke, a sail-
or, [9] and a prostitute are seated on a train station bench.
Two verbal statements in this scene--one an exchange, one
an announcement--provide further evidence of De Palma's
careful use of ambiguity in the film.

          The sailor and prostitute make arrangements for a
liaison at the rear of the station.   We follow them to a row
of phone booths in a corner and into a booth where the prostitute (obscured by the phone booth door) fellates the sailor.
He prematurely ejaculates and, instead of the previously-
agreed-upon thirty dollars, throws a ten dollar bill at the
woman.   "What about my thirty dollars?" she yells.   De
Palma provides the sailor with a pornographic pun as a rejoinder: "You blew it, baby."

          Watching the proceedings from an adjacent booth (an
appropriate spot considering his wiretapping activities and
assumption of phone employee's garb), Burke makes an as-
signation with the prostitute.   Presumably, he intends to kill
her to keep the persona of the Liberty Bell murderer alive
(considering that all three of Burke's victims--McRyan, Mary
Robert, and Sally--are guilty of sexual dalliance, there is
also the hint that sexual repression plays as large a part in
Burke's homicidal motivations as political expediency).   The
prostitute starts to walk to the women's bathroom before her
meeting with Burke, not realizing that he is walking right behind her.   Leaning over the stall next to hers, Burke garrotes
the woman just as the station's train announcer is heard saying, "Last call for the Broadway Limited," a rather appropriate statement considering that we are presently witnessing
this call girl's last "call."   If we again revert to a colloquial
reading, this woman could also be referred to as "a cheap
broad" (this is doubtless Burke's view of her and Mary and
Sally); we may then interpret the announcement as meaning
that now that she is dead, this "broad['s] way" will be extremely "limited."

Perhaps the cruelest verbal irony in the film is its use of the word and concept of "wires." Jack tells Sally that he put "a wire" on the policeman whom he outfitted for sound transmission. When Freddy's "bug" is discovered by the mobster, the recording wire is transformed into a murder weapon: Freddy is hanged with it. Later, a similar transformation from an action centering on a recording wire to one involving a murderous garrote appears when Burke chokes the "wired for sound" Sally with his wristwatch wire garrote. The circumstances of Freddy's murder are virtually reproduced in Sally's death, with Jack repeating his role as the distant, helpless technician who can do nothing to prevent the demise of the person he has outfitted electronically. Freddy and Sally, playing out Jack's commitment to gadgetry, live by the wire; as a consequence, they die by it as well.[10]

Although Jack is obviously BLOW OUT's central figure, it is the characters of Sally and Burke who supply most of the film's thrills and who are consequently given the largest number of fateful statements. Sally and Burke both make assertions that without their knowledge reveal essential, often fateful information. Within BLOW OUT's murky universe, neither character can decode the ambiguous meanings of their utterances, as though each of them were being manipulated like a pawn in some game within which they are privileged to see only a small piece of the total action.

After waiting a while for Donohue's call, Jack tells Sally that he thinks there is something wrong with his phone (he unfortunately does not consider that someone may be tapping his phone and recording his conversations, a serious omission for a man who is supposed to be knowledgeable about wiring people and setting up body taps). Sally replies, "Maybe the phone company is in on the conspiracy too," a chillingly accurate statement given Burke's assumption of telephone employee guise and his tapping of Jack's phone.

Later, when Burke ties up Karp's film with Jack's recording tape and throws it into the river, Sally tells him that "Jack's gonna kill you," the colloquial phrase revealing--in the light of later events--a startling prescience.

[Opposite:] Two kinds of "wires" from BLOW OUT. At top, Jack Terri (John Travolta) wires undercover cop Freddy for sound while Detective Mackey watches. Below, Burke (John Lithgow) with his special wire garrote.

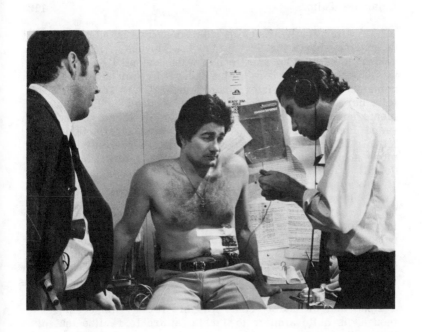

After finally revealing his homicidal intentions to Sally (a goal he signals by drawing on his gloves), Burke, reinvoking something he said to her when she still believed he was Donohue, tells her "we're going to cover the fireworks, remember?" A bit later, cautioning Sally to keep quiet, he tells her, "One more sound and you're dead." Both statements come true: the first in reverse (it is Burke and Sally --and Jack--who are covered with fireworks reflections at BLOW OUT's end), the second literally, since Sally's "one more sound" (her last scream) immediately precedes her death.

It is to Burke's discredit that when, posing as Donohue, he tells Sally they're being watched ("I think we're being followed"), he also says, "no problem." True, Jack's pursuit of Burke and Sally remains "no problem" for a while, although Burke fails to realize that just as he tapped Jack's phone, so too could Jack retaliate by "tapping" Sally in order to keep track of the woman's whereabouts. This is a serious oversight for the equipment-minded (guns, recorders) Burke, a lapse that ultimately costs him his life. This error, though, is quite similar to Jack's failure to realize that his "tapped" policeman might sweat and foul up his equipment. Ultimately, both Jack and Burke are revealed as heedless of other people's lives. Jack subverts the police undercover operation, indirectly causing a man's death. He wires Sally, using the "tap" to locate her when she is threatened with murder, although the device's initial and sole purpose was to protect himself from being "fucked" and his evidence from being misappropriated. It is only during BLOW OUT's finale, when Jack, in emotional pain, tries to drown out the noise of Sally's scream, that he apparently begins to show some compassion for other people.[11] By this time, though, it is a bit late to do anything about his victims. Like Burke, Jack victimizes relatively innocent characters; the two men can be seen as complementary characters, different in their politics perhaps, but quite similar in the way that they use people and mechanisms to achieve their desired political ends.

BLOW OUT employs a number of intentionally exaggerated cinematic devices to add pure entertainment value to the film. To mention just one example: Jack's high-speed ride down the middle of the Liberty Day parade--with spectators, police, and marchers jumping out of the way of his speeding jeep just in time--is a fine example of the patently artificial chase scene, with its souped-up pace and impossible escapes.

The tragedy of a man totally reliant on electronics: John
Travolta in BLOW OUT.

This sense of artifice for the sake of fun disappears
with the traditional De Palma use of the 360-degree pan. As
in previous films (most notably the end of OBSESSION and the
pas de deux in CARRIE), the pan is used to communicate a
feeling of deliriousness, in this case a vertiginous helpless-
ness. Jack discovers at one point that all of his studio tapes
have been erased (a task, performed by Burke, which is fore-
shadowed when we see a bulky tape eraser in the agent's car,
but which is, nevertheless, virtually impossible given the number of Jack's tapes and the amount of time that Burke had
available to him). As Jack goes from tape recorder to tape
recorder, threading up tapes that all turn out to be blank, the
camera pans around the room, now discovering the machines
playing back totally garbled sounds, now catching the anxious
Jack with a distraught look on his face. Additionally, the
pan--like the camera movement around Winslow in PHANTOM
OF THE PARADISE--describes a solipsistic circle around
Jack that nicely represents his inability to deal with people
on anything other than a non-human, electronic basis. Later,
when Jack loses Sally in the train station, the camerawork
once again reflects his tragic self-centeredness and impotence
by panning around him, this time affirming his closed-in existence and present pitiable inability to discover the young
woman's whereabouts.

     BLOW OUT's final set piece finds Jack, having stabbed
Burke to death with the ice pick, cradling the dead Sally in
his arms. With the Liberty Day fireworks blazing all around
them, the slow motion camera catches this tragic political
pietà: the innocent in the arms of the young man who will
live with his guilt for the rest of his life. It is this still-
life picture of Jack and Sally--not the glimpses of the life-
less, regimented wooden dummy Liberty Day celebrants who
stood so rigidly while the animated Jack rushed to Sally's
defense--that De Palma gives us as a chromo of liberty, as
though to say that here in the United States, deliverance from
corruption is impossible; the innocent will always suffer,
while meaningless rituals (like the Liberty Day events) only
commemorate the emptiness of our commitment to true freedom and candor in all of our relations, be they personal or
political.

     The setting for this scene--with Jack and Sally fronting
a huge American flag while the fireworks detonate--calls to
mind the last stanza of "The Star Spangled Banner": "And
the rockets' red glare, the bombs bursting in air, gave proof
through the night, that our flag was still there." In this case,

though, the giant flag behind Jack and Sally and the libertarian
ideal that it supposedly stands for are mocked by the situation
of the two people in front of it.   Sally's death confirms that
Jack's all-or-nothing view of liberty (thus his appropriate
crash into a store window that depicts the hanging of Nathan
Hale and displays part of Hale's "give me liberty or give me
death" speech) is irreconcilable with the country's present
political climate.   With politics beyond redemption, there is
no possibility for the revelation of the truth about anything,
be it the murder of a candidate (McRyan), the death of an
innocent young woman (Mary, Sally), or the correct identification of a local murderer.

        In the end, Jack abandons his political commitment and
returns to his essentially meaningless job, packaging repetitive terror (exemplified in Independence Films' endlessly derivative film titles such as Blood Beach, Blood Beach II,
Bordello of Blood) while the country's real terror, its bias
in favor of lies instead of truth, evasion of facts instead of
confrontations with them, continues unabated.   As a final,
black joke irony (De Palma can't seem to resist placing "top-
pers" at the ends of his films), the despondent Jack--who has
withdrawn once again into an emotional coldness reflected in
the winter setting of his penultimate appearance, and who repeatedly listens to the tape of Sally's last struggles, her
screams and then her death--lifts her scream off the tape
and inserts it into the shower scene in Coed Frenzy.12

        We thus return to BLOW OUT's beginning, as if the
film were an endless loop doubling back on itself like the assassination investigations which are riddled with dead ends
and non-sequiturs.   Not only has Jack regressed to being
apolitical, but he is revealed as emotionally coarse enough
to take the screams of a woman whom he obviously cared
for and throw them into a tawdry, grade-Z horror production, as though to say, "Not only do I not care, but this is
an appropriate conclusion to all of my struggles.   This is
the way it is in America: the pure [and Sally, as played by
Allen, seems beguilingly pure despite the shady deals she
has been involved in] must inevitably be corrupted, while the
guilty go free" (McRyan's pristine reputation is still intact;
Jack is still alive).   What better icon of a corrupt America
than a real (within the film's fiction) cry for help and deliverance locked forever inside a patently artificial production
like Coed Frenzy, a film featuring a phony killer (not real
like Burke) and phony victims (unlike Mary and Sally)?   BLOW
OUT leaves us with the impression of a great soul's entrap-

ment within a corrupt body, as fitting a metaphor for America as anyone in contemporary filmmaking is likely to give us for quite a while.

NOTES

1. With its theme of a withdrawn sound technician becoming involved in a murder plot as a result of a recording he makes, BLOW OUT calls up memories of Coppola's THE CONVERSATION, another Watergate-influenced work.   Both films have the protagonist move from alienation to involvement and then, after a climactic cinematic paroxysm, back to alienation, resulting in a strikingly similar tone.

    In theme and title, BLOW OUT invites comparison with Antonioni's BLOWUP.   Both films involve a piece of evidence (in BLOWUP a photo, in BLOW OUT an audio-visual record) of a murder that is examined more and more closely in an attempt to yield information about the event.   However, in neither film does the examination of the evidence lead the investigator any closer to the truth.   Like a photograph progressively enlarged so that after a while the only information yielded is a view of photographic grain (a point made by Gerrit Graham's female companion while he traced wound marks on her during HI, MOM), the increasingly acute examination of evidence in each film only leads to further obscuring of the crimes' perpetrators.   The message in both BLOWUP and BLOW OUT is clear: we can never hope to possess the "total truth" about any situation through a calculated, scientific evaluation of supposedly objective evidence.   Only human empathy can aid us in approaching "the facts."

2. This latter claim is probably false, since if he didn't intend to kill the Governor, why was Burke fingering his wire garrote--a gesture performed immediately prior to each of the murders he commits--just before the Governor's car came into view?

3. If this statement didn't make it obvious enough that the McRyan Commission would from the beginning be biased, one only has to take into account Mackey's statement about Jack's work with the King Commission. "You were responsible for putting a lot of good cops away," the policeman says.   Jack's job doubtless resulted in the conviction of guilty policemen; that Mac-

key calls these men "good cops" is quite fitting for
one who must himself be corrupt, and who is already
prepared to condone the premature findings of an obviously biased commission.

4. The fact that BLOW OUT's murderous actions take place
    in "the city of brotherly love" is an example of char-
    acteristic De Palma irony.

5. Actually, Burke--an obsessive conservative with his "I
    Love Liberty" button (whose acronym, ILL, gives us
    a clue to his psychological state) and red, white, and
    blue (the appropriate color scheme of the entire film)
    tie--is in some depraved way affirming his belief in
    democracy by stenciling this design on his victims.
    To borrow and slightly alter Patrick Henry's phrase
    (which in an unaltered form is, as we shall see, di-
    rectly applicable to Jack), Burke gives his victims
    "liberty and death."

6. In this sense the film's plot and Jack's character owe a
    great deal to Truffaut's SHOOT THE PIANO PLAYER.

7. Symbolic placement is used in two other scenes with sim-
    ilar effect. In one, which takes place in a train sta-
    tion, Burke and a prostitute he is soon to murder are
    separated by a sailor, who represents an impediment
    to Burke's homicidal tendencies that is soon to be re-
    moved. We have already seen Jack waiting at home
    for Donohue's call, sitting between his telephone (which
    is in the foreground, since the call is all-important)
    and his television. Neither object, though, aids Jack's
    inquiry into McRyan's death. The expected phone call
    from Donohue never comes (Burke is jamming the
    phone), while the hints about McRyan and Burke on
    the television go unnoticed by Jack. He is, as his
    placement in the frame suggests, caught in the middle
    between the two sources of information, neither of
    which is of any help to him in his investigation.

8. Interestingly, there are three occupants in the car Freddy
    is riding in: Freddy, the mobster, and Freddy's po-
    lice captain, who is the man Freddy is attempting to
    entrap. This initial exposure to corruption in the up-
    per levels of the police force (the actor playing the
    role is identified in the credits as a "corrupt Cap-
    tain") prepares us for Jack's understandable, albeit
    incorrect, claim that it was the police who erased
    the tape he gives to Mackey. In fact, Jack probably
    believes that Mackey himself was responsible for the
    erasure, given the policeman's involuntary presence
    when Freddy was being wired. De Palma is doubtless

   also counting on the viewer's applying this distrust of
   officials to Jack Matters as well, whose true feelings
   about "fair play" seem highly suspicious.

9.   The sailor is identified as being "on liberty," thus set-
     ting up a link with the Liberty Bell murderer, who is
     soon to kill the prostitute the sailor is presently in-
     volved with.

10. Jack's rushing on foot to save Sally reminds us of his
     two claims about the kind of man he is. In the hos-
     pital, he refers to himself as "a sound man." In the
     bar at the train station, he tells Sally that he is "a
     leg man." Here, at BLOW OUT's end, he "legs it"
     towards Sally in response to the sounds she makes in
     calling out his name.

11. Even this emotional display may be less an example of
     compassion than an attempt to reject the entire painful
     episode instead of learning from it. If anything, given
     Jack's rather callous act at BLOW OUT's end, the lat-
     ter interpretation seems to be the most likely.

12. The repeated studio playbacks of the scream at BLOW
     OUT's end prompt Jack to place his hands over his
     ears, a useless gesture since the screams will doubt-
     less continue to echo in his memory for quite a while.

Chapter Ten: THE CRAFT OF SUSPENSE:
An Interview with Brian De Palma

BLISS: Let me start out by asking you a few questions
about some of your films.   I assumed in my chapter on HI,
MOM that the Be Black, Baby theatre production in the film
was actually unrehearsed.

DE PALMA: Oh no, it was rehearsed for almost three
weeks, but it was like a very open improvisation in which
you have a troupe of actors and a troupe of audience people
who have been improvising along certain lines for quite a
long time, and you've worked out a certain kind of set piece
and drama for them to play.   In fact, it's all scripted.   But
once the thing starts, they just go with the way it's going.
I specifically got a very good documentary filmmaker to just
shoot it like a documentary to follow the action.   A good documentary filmmaker will watch how action unfolds and immediately go to how it's playing.   Bob Elstrom, who's excellent
at this, just followed it, and that's why it looks so real.

B: Then the people who came to the performance in the film
were actors?

D: Absolutely.   They were actors or people who had worked
in an acting group for quite a while.   The one thing I did not
do is that I never introduced the really mean blacks into the
group until we actually shot it; the audience had never been
exposed to these two guys before and they were really mean.
They were so mean that when I first started to rehearse I

119

just sent them home and said, fellas, we'll save you for the shooting, because they were so hostile.   They hated me and hated what I was doing and hated the whole idea, called us white motherfuckers and were just going to beat the shit out of us.   So consequently, when I brought them on, the audience people were scared.

B: That's what I wanted to know, because it looks like the "audience" didn't know what was going to happen.

D: Only in that sequence in the elevator were they up against something they had never seen before.   But they had worked so much and improvised so much that they could go with it wherever it went.

B: In any case, their trust was violated; even the cameraman was threatened.

D: Yes, those guys were cruel.

B: GET TO KNOW YOUR RABBIT is so different from the rest of your work.   I pointed out in my book that it's almost completely out of line with everything else you've done.   Was this change of tone your doing or was the script something that was brought to you by Warner Bros. ?

D: It was a project developed at Warner Bros. that Tommy Smothers was casting which I decided to do because all of the projects that I was trying to get done at that time were not getting done.   I was under a contract to Filmways Pictures and they owned a lot of my things like SISTERS and PHANTOM and HOME MOVIES and I knew they were never going to be produced at Filmways so I took the job of GET TO KNOW YOUR RABBIT in order to buy my way out of my Filmways contract.

B: Does that mean that you're not particularly happy with the project?

D: I'm not happy with it because I couldn't control it.   It's one of the few pictures that got completely out of my control. The ending is not mine and the way that I wanted to end it was never done.

B: How did you want to end it?

D: I thought that the Tommy Smothers character should have his moment of truth where he vanquishes the John Astin character. He's such a nebbish all through the movie--I wanted him to suddenly realize he's being co-opted by all of these forces and suddenly rebel against them, which he sort of does in the movie but in a very lackadaisical way, not a way in which the audience gets excited in the sense that the worm turns and gets back at all of these people who have been doing these terrible things to him. I wanted him to humiliate the Turnbull character, destroy his corporation, and then go back on the road and be a tap-dancing magician.

B: Instead, he just disappears.

D: Yes, he just quits; he just says, "Well, I'm not going to do this any more," and walks out again. Why didn't he just walk out when he walked in? There's no reason for it.

B: I was really disappointed in the film because I watched your first three films in sequence, GREETINGS, then HI, MOM, and then there was this abrupt change of tone in the way the film moved and the way it ended. There was something sluggish about the entire ending that reflected back on the rest of the film as though you had been cheated.

D: That's true. That's an instance where I'm directing somebody else's material and trying to realize it to the best of my abilities. I don't think that the style and the texture of the writer's material worked; I discovered that when I was preparing the picture and even, in fact, when I was shooting it, but I couldn't get anybody to listen to me.

B: There's a piece on SISTERS by Robin Wood that says that SISTERS is the first feminist film to come out of Hollywood; it's a psychological and structuralist reading of the film. It talks about the knife as a phallic object.

D: I don't like to get into that kind of reading into things. I remember talking to Robin and asking him questions about this. I finally said, look, that wasn't what I was doing when I made the movie; you may see these things but it's beyond me. But I do feel in a sense that I deal with contemporary feminist characters, and this accusation that I make movies just to have women get chopped up and killed to me is silly, because a lot of my movies have women protagonists and they're not the usual wife who is making coffee for the lead character or is going to bed with him or is any frill in the movie--you know, a little sweet music, a little flesh. Most

of my women characters are very active, very strong; they
dominate the action for the most part. In SISTERS all they
do is dominate the action. In DRESSED TO KILL all of the
men are practically like women in normal films. So whether
they're prostitutes or girls making money on the side by setting up candidates or actresses or newspaper reporters--to
me they are contemporary women and are aggressively pursuing their goals.

B: The next-to-last scene in CARRIE appears to have been
shot in reverse; was there any other effect aside from dis-
location that you wanted to achieve there, because it's very
strange.

D: Yes, it's very eerie. I did it five different ways. I
had more action going backwards. I had a lot of traffic going backwards, I had people walking backwards up the street,
I had Sue's mother walking backwards at one point. I had
everything going backwards, and then every time I did a different take I kept on pulling elements out until it was just
right on the edge where you think something is amiss but
you don't know exactly what it is.

B: All you can see if you really watch ...

D: ... is just the one car going in reverse.

B: Sissy Spacek said in a recent interview that when she
worked with you on CARRIE she noticed that you were always diagramming things and that you were very methodical.
The person who conducted the interview said that didn't leave
much room for creativity on the part of the actors. But it
occurred to me that that's the same thing Hitchcock used to
do: storyboard the films out before shooting. Is that pretty
much the way that you work?

D: There's a little difference because I diagram things out
to give the movie a certain visual design. Not only did Hitchcock diagram things out, he had the script so locked in that
they went out and shot exactly what was on the script. I tend
to be a little looser than that because I feel that it's important to give a kind of warmth and life to the dramatic performances. So the actors play around with the scenes a little
bit and take them in different directions, within certain set
limitations. I think that's good because it keeps the depth
and heart of the characters viable and real as opposed to my
walking in there with something that's precisely written out

and giving the actors no kind of flexibility. I also tend to
shoot character scenes very simply so that it gives the actors a chance to be able to move around and say different
things and be able to play with the material.

B: You've used the split screen effect in SISTERS and in
CARRIE. Yet for some reason, even though it only appears
in those two films and in BLOW OUT, people seem to get
the feeling that it's all over in your work and that you do
nothing but split screens.

D: Yes, I know.

B: In BLOW OUT you seem to turn the device on its head
and use it for a very simple telephone conversation, which
is precisely the way it used to be used in 30s films, which
had the jagged edge between the characters on the phone.
Does this mean you're going to repudiate the device?

D: I used it in the title sequence of BLOW OUT and I used
a lot of split diopters in the film, so that you have two focal
points, a front and back focal point, like when John Lithgow
is looking at Allen's picture while in the background a young
woman is descending an escalator. I use the split screen as
a technique; I don't beat it to death. I wasn't particularly
trying to tell the critics anything in that BLOW OUT scene.
With a telephone conversation, you can either intercut to
each character--show one side and then the other side--or
sometimes you can show them together. I was trying to
show the connection of the two locations. Travolta and Allen hear the siren in both places; I wanted to differentiate
between the two background locations at the same time, which
I achieved by using the split screen.

B: You had the Dolby stereo going there too, didn't you?

D: Yes, I had the sound split on either side of the screen,
but the siren is very critical because it blots out a very important piece of expositional information, which of course nobody gets: the fact that Sally says that she doesn't know what
this television reporter looks like because she never watches
television. Now, just as she's saying that, the siren is going
off and Jack is looking away from the phone, and he comes
back and says "What?" and she proceeds on.

B: Was HOME MOVIES a film that you had a commitment to
do when you were Director-in-Residence at Sarah Lawrence
College?

D: No, it was something I created all on my own. After I
finished THE FURY, I traveled around the country a lot listening to kids talk about how you get started. I though the
best thing I could do was to show how you put together a low-
budget feature, the way I did when I was a young director.
So I proceeded to call up a school which I took a master's
degree at and said, I want to do a course on how to make a
low-budget feature, and they said fine, and I said well, we're
going to start next week. So we got a lot of students and we
just started to do a low-budget feature; the whole course was
a kind of discovery of how you go about making a low-budget
film. I broke the kids up into production people and screen-
writing people and all kinds of areas that they wanted to get
into. We worked on the script and we worked on putting the
production together and raising the money and casting and
everything you have to do; it was a long, arduous process.
To raise the money we had 27 different deals going, and one
of them finally came through, just as in all these low-budget
features. We ran over budget and we had to get more money:
all the classical problems you have in making a low-budget
feature.

B: What was the budget?

D: It was budgeted at 220 and it came in at about 320.

B: Are you familiar with an interview that Michael Caine
gave out just before DRESSED TO KILL opened, an interview
which I assume was conducted before Caine did the film, because he says that he would never take a part that violated
his sophisticated veneer, and yet it seemed to me that in
that particular film, the part you're using him for peels that
away. He's this sleek, well-dressed psychiatrist but he's
really a very strange, disturbed character underneath. Were
you aware of the fact that he was making those kind of comments?

D: I've read a lot of interviews with Michael and I never got
the impression that he felt this part violated his veneer. In
fact, he was always very enthusiastic about the script and the
part right from the beginning, even in subsequent interviews.
I think he began to pull away from it when he got involved
with THE HAND and he started to say, well, I'll never make
another horror picture. But he's been very consistent in how
he felt about DRESSED TO KILL, in what he said to me and
how he approached the material. He had great fun playing
the dressed character; I don't believe in any sense he would
think that it was violating whatever image he had set up.

B: The Monthly Film Bulletin says that you cheat in DRESSED
TO KILL by showing Caine in a split-screen shot watching a
show about transsexuals while the blonde, whom you find out
later is a policewoman, is walking along the street, and that
the assumption for the audience at that point is that Caine
can't be the killer.

D: Of course. What's cheating about that?

B: Nothing that I can see, but they say you're cheating the
audience by showing them that this can't be Caine.

D: Why is that any worse than having PSYCHO's Mrs. Bates
stuffed in a rocking chair in a window? Or having this loud
conversation between Norman and his mother, where he must
be shouting at the top of his lungs in order that Marion hears?

B: Yes, the same kind of thing happens in SISTERS. You
get the conversation between the two sisters: you see the
shadow, and you hear the two voices, and people said--and
I anticipated this in the book because I wanted to cover this
point--that you're being tricked there into believing that there
really are two separate, corporeal sisters.

D: Why not, if it's something that's not so wild that when
the trick is revealed you say, "Awwww." I don't think that's
the case in DRESSED TO KILL. I think people get confused
a lot in DRESSED TO KILL; I've read a number of reviews
in which people believe that Bobbie gets knocked down by that
cabbie.

B: It looks like it.

D: Of course it looks like it, but it's the policewoman. But
people somehow think it's Bobbie and they say, how does she
get back to the house so fast, when in reality "she" was always at the house.

B: THE FURY is a tremendous amount of fun to watch: it's
like somebody is let loose in a toy shop. It's obvious from
a lot of the scenes, especially the scenes with the cops and
the Mother Nuckells sequence, that much of it's just being
played for laughs. Yet people say there's nothing funny going on here. Why do you think all of this comedy is missed?

D: For some reason audiences just can't seem to accept
comic relief scenes in movies of this nature; it's somehow
unacceptable in their artistic parameters but god knows

there's nothing new about it. I was interested to see how
an AMERICAN WEREWOLF IN LONDON would do because
Landis is running horror and comedy right next to each other
there. I liked it; I thought the movie was very bold, but I
think audiences for the most part, unless you do it cleverly,
are thrown by it, and critics have no idea how to judge it--
they think you're playing with them for some reason, as
though how dare you have a comic scene in the midst of all
this murder and mayhem?

B: That may be it. You're getting serious, you're having
people killed and you don't, in a lot of people's opinion, have
any right to joke around. Yet you get that black comedy all
through PSYCHO.

D: Absolutely.

B: But it's a funny thing--PSYCHO got panned the way a lot
of your films got panned early on, as just being a slasher
film with the same attitude towards sexuality: the woman
who indulges in sex gets killed. So why don't you just tell
people to quit picking on you?

D: Well, I've said that, and it has no effect on them. I've
said, this has all been done before, it's been written about
before, and then they say well, you're not Hitchcock.

B: Yes, that's it; it sounds like sacrilege when you compare
yourself.

D: Exactly--how dare you? This man that they've been panning probably 60 years of his life and all of a sudden they
decide he's a master.

B: There was a stand-in the shower scene for Janet Leigh
in PSYCHO and there was a stand-in for Angie Dickinson in
DRESSED TO KILL's shower sequence. Was that because
Dickinson insisted on a stand-in or did you put that in there
as another Hitchcock parallel? When I saw the film I thought,
that's not Dickinson; she probably refused to do it. Is that
true?

D: No, it wasn't a matter of her refusing to do it. But
what's the point of having Angie Dickinson in there while
you're shooting tight shots of nipples and hips and pubic areas; it's a waste of time as far as I can see. Why not get
somebody else in there to do those tight shots; that's the way

I always felt about it and there was nothing more to it than
that. Who wants to sit in a shower with water draining on
you while you're shooting like this?

B: Matched doubles, composite pairs of characters, appear
quite often in your films: Sue and Chris in CARRIE, Danielle and Dominique in SISTERS, the two psychic youngsters
in THE FURY, Winslow and Swan in PHANTOM OF THE
PARADISE, and so on. Is this type of characterization
something that you saw and liked in Hitchcock's work or is
it just a quality that naturally emerges in your films?

D: I wouldn't say that was a conscious choice. A lot of
times you deal with schizophrenic characters, as in SISTERS,
and in CARRIE those characters were created by Stephen King
for the most part--there are the good girls and the bad girls,
the good guy and the bad guy, the nice teachers and the bad
teachers. I wouldn't say that that was a conscious choice.
Mainly, though, you choose the material because you like
certain things in it. Now whether you say, "I'm going to
have matched doubles in all my movies"--well, it doesn't
really happen that way.

B: I have a friend who said that there is something unpleasant about all of your films--that when you go into them you
feel trapped, and that the universe operating in those films
is filled full of threat. Is this quality something that you
think is going to continue in your future work?

D: Well, I don't believe essentially in letting people off the
hook, letting good triumph or basically resolving things, because I think we live in an era in which things are unresolved
and terrible events happen and you never forget them. So
that's true to some extent.

B: Even though there was both color and black and white
available to him, Hitchcock sometimes would opt for color,
sometimes for black and white, as in PSYCHO being shot in
black and white followed by THE BIRDS being shot in color.
Have you ever felt that you'd like to work in black and white
as opposed to color or are you under pressure by the studios
to have your productions come out in color?

D: I've never felt particularly that I would have to work in
color. The only thing that I think would make real sense is
if you were shooting a film noir picture. They seem to work
a lot better in that kind of harsh black and white. But you

could probably accomplish that in color if it were done correctly.   I think black and white in RAGING BULL works quite well.   That's a good choice because of the fight scenes and the blood and all that; that makes sense to me.   It also helps with the period.

B: What I've noticed in CARRIE, and in all of your scripts, is that there's no excess, no scenes that break the films' continuity.   Do you do a lot of paring of your scripts to achieve that type of economy?

D: I pride myself on the fact that my movies are very lean and play very well.   To some extent I feel that maybe I should have more character scenes in which people sit down and expose themselves more to the audience, but I see so much of that in other movies and it bores me a lot because it's done badly a lot of the time.   I'm very concerned with the pace of the movie, that it keep moving, that the story keep turning, and that a lot of unexpected things happen.   In most movies that I go to you're there for three minutes and you know exactly what's going to happen for the next two hours--you know the story, you know how the characters are going to evolve; that's all given to you in about three or four minutes.   I tend always to try to keep the audience not knowing what's going to happen and not giving them the expected scene.

B: Most of the people who read my newspaper piece on BLOW OUT said, enough already, you went to see the film four times, that's why you saw all of these references; it's meaningless for the average viewer.   What should people be seeing in that film?   How aware do you think the audience should be?

D: Well, there's a whole subtext there but you don't have to see it for the movie to work.   I feel that a film has to make a direct contact with your visual sensibility, and if you sit there and think about it and stand back from it, then you're missing the experience that's right in front of your eyes; that's why you get these misinformed reviews all the time, because people are not watching the movie, they're not letting the movie work on them the way it should.   They're sitting there thinking about the things that it's about and not just watching it.

B: You can do both at once.

D: Absolutely you can do both at once, but when you go into
a movie you just want to go with it, you don't want to sit
there and start deciphering it.   I think a movie should be
like a rollercoaster ride: you should get on and go for the
ride first.   When you want to criticize a movie or when I
see a friend's movie and he wants me to say what I think
about it, I usually go see it a couple of times because the
first time I don't want to think about what it's about.   I just
want to see if it works; then I can start thinking about well,
that scene's too long, and why does that character do this,
and sort of act more like a critic.

B: Have you gotten any political reactions to BLOW OUT?

D: You mean political groups?

B: I mean anybody who says, who the hell do you think you
are with these Kennedy allusions?   Here's another womanizing
Senator who drives off a bridge with, as his aide puts it, "his
hand up a girl's dress."

D: Nothing.

B: Surprising.

D: No, because they dismissed it as a horror picture which
doesn't mean anything in political terms.

B: BLOW OUT has been referred to as a slasher film, this
in spite of the fact that it is totally critical of the murderous
goings-on it depicts.   How do you deal with this kind of reaction?

D: That's what I don't understand.   The movie is reviewed
as though people are not watching the screen.   They talk
about the violence in it; there is no violence in it.

B: Well, not particularly; there's a stabbing.

D: There is one close up, which is very dark, of one icepick going into John Lithgow.   As far as explicit violence is
concerned, there is nil.

B: I think this is the kind of trouble you're going to continue
to run into, and this is something that happened to Hitchcock,
too.   Hitchcock's violence isn't that explicit.   I show PSYCHO

to my film class students, and I show them an extract from
it again, and I ask them, "How many times is Marion Crane
stabbed?" Some people say "three" and some people say
"twenty," but when I slow the film down they see that the
knife never touches her at all. I think what people don't
like about BLOW OUT, and what they transfer to you in the
form of criticisms of you as a violent filmmaker, is that
there's an undercurrent of violence in your work, not explicit, but nevertheless more disturbing.

D: Well, that's fine, there's nothing wrong with that, but
my work is thrown in with THE TEXAS CHAINSAW MASSA-
CRE and written about as though I'm chopping people up,
eviscerating people, that heads are rolling down stairs. I'll
never forget arguing with the head of the MPAA about DRESSED
TO KILL. There was not that much explicit violence in
DRESSED TO KILL, and he said, "This picture is beauti-
fully done but I'm going to give it an X because of how violent it is." I said, where, what are you talking about, it
just was not that violent. Because of your artistry, because
you can imply violence without showing it, you are censored.
That's a very disturbing situation for me. I have no qualms
about it: my movies are well advertised in the sense that
you know you're going in there for some kind of wild rollercoaster ride. You go to see a movie called DRESSED TO
KILL, with somebody holding a straight razor, you know
you're in trouble.

B: I thought it was about a haberdasher (laughter). Well,
DRESSED TO KILL finally got an R, though; it didn't get an
X.

D: Only because I took some material out.

B: What was removed?

D: Interestingly enough, in the videocassette that's out now,
they have the international version, which has everything in it.

B: What's missing from the American release version?

D: There was a lot more caressing of pubic hair and breasts.

B: In the shower scene?

D: Yes. A lot more humping.

B: Under the covers!

D: No, in the shower scene. In the elevator, there's a
closeup of the razor cutting her throat, there's a closeup
of the razor cutting her cheek ...

B: I really can't see how that could be worse than that cut
across the palm. It's just a repetition of it.

D: Well, wait until you see it; it has a lot more sock to it.
It makes a big difference to me. I think if you're going to
murder somebody horribly in an elevator, you'd better really
murder her horribly.

B: But I don't see any difference in terms of rating between
one slash and three slashes.

D: Neither do I. That's what I would argue, but you're
really arguing pubic hair against four fucks against a closeup of a razor. You know, I'll take out one razor if you keep
two fucks ...

B: Two fucks for one razor, one pubic hair ...

D: Exactly--it's like a negotiation.

B: In your films, revulsion and sexuality are virtually always linked; at least from SISTERS on, only William Katt
and Sissy Spacek in CARRIE, Allen and Travolta in BLOW
OUT, and Liz and Peter in DRESSED TO KILL promise
some form of productive relationships, but those relationships are never shown: it's cut short in CARRIE, you don't
see it in DRESSED TO KILL, and of course nothing is going
to happen in BLOW OUT because the Nancy Allen character
dies. This inherent pessimism underlies all of the films--
is this a necessary aspect of what I've referred to as your
film universe?

D: It's hard to say exactly that, well, sex leads to death,
or if you do something bad sexually some terrible thing is
going to occur later on. I would have to think about each
film quite specifically. To me, it is a device that works;
I don't think of it as a philosophy. You know, if you make
movies that deal with the devil, audiences tend to get behind
them as opposed to having some kind of evil government agency
as the threat. Somehow they accept the fact that the devil is

evil and they accept devil concepts rather than bad organiza-
tion concepts. I've always felt that sex and guilt worked very
well; it's a device that people respond to. If the characters
do something sexually bad, then the audience is willing to
have the characters pay for it on some level or other. Now,
that may be because I believe that or because I think that it
works. I don't consider myself a puritan who says, if you
have illicit sex you're going to die. But I use that device
a lot in my movies mainly because I think audiences believe
it and because I think it works.

In DRESSED TO KILL, the sort of zipless fuck--you
know she's going to have to pay for that. In CARRIE, again,
what I have to fall back on essentially is, that's the idea of
the book. Now whether I was attracted to it for that is something else, but the fact is that "first the blood, then the
boys," that's Stephen King's statement, it isn't mine. But
I use the emergence of teenage sexuality as a cataclysmic
event in the lives of the people in Bates High School.

As I say, I think it's like believing in the devil; I just
think people believe it: they believe in pure evil, they believe sex is bad. You try to deal with things that an audience can identify with on a visceral level and I feel that's
what they identify with to some extent. People say, "Why
do women get slashed in his films, what does he have against
women?" I just think that when women are in a perilous situation, audiences identify with them more than men because
they look more helpless. People say, "Well, he's out to kill
women," but when you have a man walking down a dark hall
you don't care as much if somebody jumps out and kills him
or threatens him.

B: Why is there nobody else doing your kind of filmmaking?
You get the grade-B garbage, the HALLOWEEN clones, the
TEXAS CHAINSAW MASSACRE type, and that's it.

D: There are just not many people working in this genre,
mainly because it's considered a B genre to begin with and
always has been. Hitchcock gave it some dignity but outside
of Hitchcock there's really no other place to fit and audiences
really haven't accepted me. Some people have, some other
people haven't. There are also not too many people prac-
ticing in this area because it's very difficult. You have to
have a tremendous visual imagination, incredible techniques.

There are very few pictures that you really watch in
the sense that they surprise you as a director. Recently, I
was talking to Steven Spielberg about this. Steven's pictures
always surprise me; there are always things going on there

that I say, wow, I wish I had thought of that! Then there's Martin Scorsese and that's about it. There are always things that shock and surprise you in these people's movies because whatever you think about the stories and the characters, the films have great visual design and some kind of unusual sensibility at work. Steven to me is like a master craftsman: his stories don't get too bizarre but as far as realizing what he's trying to do, I don't think he has an equal. And Marty has such a bizarre sensibility, so unique; his stories are so unusual. But outside of that, there's nobody coming along that I'm really too interested in watching. We've been talking about how disappointing THE SHINING was. What's happened to Stanley Kubrick? You used to rush out to see a Stanley Kubrick picture. Now, forget it. When we were young directors, and would go to see a Stanley Kubrick picture, Stanley would do something and you'd say, Jesus, that's incredible, what a vision! I don't feel that any more.

B: Some people have referred to you as the contemporary master of suspense. Are you comfortable with that designation?

D: Except for the inevitable, endless comparisons with Hitchcock, there's nothing wrong with being a master of anything-- master of the macabre, master of suspense; it's just a label you're stuck with. I'm proud of the fact that I probably make better suspense movies than anybody else. Maybe I can do some other things.

B: What other things would you like to do? A musical comedy like Scorsese?

D: I'm interested in movies with more interesting character relationships. Right now I'm working on two things: a movie based on the Yablonski murders called ACT OF VENGEANCE and a modern adaptation of SIERRA MADRE dealing with cocaine.

B: Those sound radically different from anything else you've done.

D: Yes, they are. I've never done anything quite like this before and I'm going to see how it works.

B: You've worked with Paul Schrader; what do you think of his work?

D: I think you're right; he writes the same script over and over again. When he had other directors directing them, somehow we made them work, but left to his own devices, with his own script, he's not been too successful because his scripts always have terrible story problems. Basically, he has a character who gets pushed around until the last scene and who then explodes. But he has a very good mind. I worked with him on a script, obviously, OBSESSION; I worked with him on his other scripts and I can see what his problems are. Unfortunately, being in Hollywood is not conducive to solving your problems.

B: Does it augment them?

D: It's just that your excesses get more excessive and your deficiencies get bigger. Everybody suffers from certain problems of being powerful and being able to do what you want, though that doesn't always necessarily make the best movie.

B: A problem of being powerful?

D: Sure, because the problem of being successful is that people in the business think everything you do is wonderful. So you can get some deranged idea that you want to make a movie about some weird subject with weird idiosyncratic characters that you like and if you're successful you'll probably get to make it. And it may be the worst movie in the world for you.

B: And then you have a lot of people around you saying, that's a great idea, Brian.

D: It's fabulous, I love it, let's do it.

B: How do you resist that?

D: It's a matter of being able to be solidly sure of your ideas and testing them in a very critical atmosphere before you go out and try to do them. In many cases you may still be wrong, but at least you won't suffer from living in a world in which everybody says that everything you do is wonderful. It's really hard to deal with the kind of input you get sometimes, even though it may be critical, because you may still go out and make a film that may not be right for you to make at the time. But it's certainly better than making a whole series of films like you're completely lost. It's better to have some feedback, to have somebody walk up to you and say, that is a terrible idea, that was the worst movie you ever made, why did you do this thing, why did you do that thing? I'm very aware of the criticism that I get from my peers and from the critical establishment and it makes me think twice about the next movie I make.

B: I would think that DRESSED TO KILL would have occasioned the most varied responses.

D: I was expecting to get totally roasted for DRESSED TO KILL.

B: Why?

D: Because it's similar to PSYCHO. But I was amazed at the kind of very good reviews that I got and the tremendous media hype and response that came out on the film. People were writing articles about it in Esquire and New York magazine, things that had never happened to me before. And then quite the opposite, I thought, well, BLOW OUT, now this is a very serious movie about a serious subject, and I got the total opposite response. Movie reviewers dismissed it as a remake of this and a copy of that and a few very astute critics discovered the picture that was there. But for the most part, it was rather negatively reviewed even though it was probably one of the most audacious movies I've ever made.

B: In what sense audacious?

D: In dealing with a kind of material that I'd never dealt with before and trying not to pander to the bloodlust of the audience, which is what I've been accused of doing many times.

B: I think those are the kind of critical double binds that people can keep you in, that if you do the type of films you've been accused of doing, the "pandering slasher films," then you're second-rate. If you try to do something contemporary, as though you actually have opinions on certain timely matters, then people think, look at this guy, he's audacious enough to try and say something about politics, well, we're going to let him have it.

D: I think you're probably right. There's no doubt to me that BLOW OUT was never taken seriously. I was trying to deal with very thematic material and a kind of character who

has a certain kind of crisis--his kind of world, his ideas--
and for the most part it was totally dismissed.

B: Travolta looks great in that last shot when he drags on
his cigarette and says "good scream, good scream," and
Pauline Kael mentioned his impressive reaction when he sees
the garroted cop.

D: It's good that the critics pick up those elements because
they're things you really work at and it's good to see that
somebody is seeing what you're doing.   But for the most
part, as far as the mass media is concerned, these aspects
are completely unnoticed.   It's amazing what happens when
you get accepted; it's usually when you're way over the hill.
Hitchcock got accepted when he was heading right over the
hill, and every movie after that point, like TORN CURTAIN
or THE BIRDS or FAMILY PLOT or MARNIE, are his worst
pictures, yet they're written about like they're masterworks.

B: I find MARNIE, and particularly FRENZY, very depress-
ing to watch; FRENZY looks and sounds like a television
movie, yet it was highly praised.

D: That's what happens to the critical establishment; it also
happens in the Hollywood community when your films become
successful.   Then, everything that you do is wonderful, even
though it may be the worst shit that you've ever cranked out
in your life.   I'm reaching into all kinds of material now to
try to see if I'll survive doing something a little different
than what I've done before.   It may be catastrophic; it may
be exactly the wrong kind of thing for me to do.

B: What will you do if it is?

D: I don't know.   I'll have to try it first.   Fortunately, I
won't be dead after I'm finished.   Needless to say, I have
all kinds of suspense and terror ideas ruminating in my
brain, but I want to try dealing with a kind of character
piece and do a thematic action type of picture--which is
where BLOW OUT was taking me--and see what happens.
     The other problem is that you have this terrible dif-
ficulty with sometimes trying to do the things you cannot do.
If you're a dancer you want to sing; if you're a singer you
want to dance, and you wind up spending your whole life saying to everybody, I know I can sing but I'm really a hell of
a dancer, and trying to show everybody what your dance steps
are and everybody says, just sing.   So that's something else
you have to consider.

B: In American Film Now, James Monaco talked about Paul
Mazursky's having enough "fuck you money" after the success
of BOB AND CAROL AND TED AND ALICE to do whatever he
wanted. Is that a possibility for you now with the success of
DRESSED TO KILL and BLOW OUT?

D: Yes, but the problem isn't having enough "fuck you money" to do what you want. What you may want to do may be
the worst thing that you do. I'm in a position to make any
picture I want to make now, but that's a terrible power because you could also make a picture with your worst ideas.
When you have that kind of power, the problem is, what do
you do with it when you have it? It's something that you have
to think about a lot.
        I try to work on areas that I'm very good at, like
suspense, that kind of psycho-sexual melodrama, things
that always attract me, and then I may be attracted to a different kind of book. I like film noir, but again, I may go
back and make DRESSED TO KILL II; I don't know. You're
not always the best judge of what you should be doing. The
trouble with our business is that you don't get good feedback.
If you make a great picture, it may be a disaster at the box-
office even though it may be the best picture you've ever
made. Kubrick made LOLITA, which is probably one of his
greatest pictures, and it was a total disaster. What does
that tell you about what you're doing?

B: Doesn't it depend on what you're measuring success by?
If you're measuring it by a film's grosses ...

D: Yes, but LOLITA got critically destroyed and economically
destroyed. Then, five, ten years later, people start to say,
what a masterpiece, how did we miss that?

B: There are some people, though, whose feelings about a
film at the time of its release are very close to those about
the film five or ten years later. Isn't it that kind of viewer
whose reactions you have to rely on--that and your own judg-
ment?

D: Well, that's what keeps you going. When you've stepped
out in a very strange area, there are a few people who see
what you're doing. You have to be able not to listen to the
horde shrieking one thing and instead listen to those few
voices that say yes, that's the direction you should be going
in. But it's very difficult sometimes. This is a profession
in which you're walking a very thin line because you know
that if you fall on your face too often, that's it, you will not

work again, you're just out.   I've grown up with too many
directors who are out, directors like Jimmy McBride, Bob
Downey, and Paul Williams--gone, they can't work.   What
could be worse than not being able to direct?

B: We had a couple of directors come out to last year's
Minneapolis Film Festival, Joseph L. Mankiewicz for one.
He's a strong director who's done a number of absolutely
brilliant films and he's certainly an extremely witty man.
I sat in on an interview with him and I said, what have you
been doing since SLEUTH, and he said, nothing, because nobody will come to me with any money.   I asked him if he
had any particular project he'd like to film and he mentioned
two very intriguing works, but he can't seem to get financing
for them.

D: That's something we all have to look forward to, the time
when you go out of vogue.

B: What will you do if that happens?

D: Better find something else to do; I hope it's when I'm 70.

BIOGRAPHICAL NOTE

Brian De Palma was born in Newark, New Jersey in 1940.
When he was about five years old, his family moved to Philadelphia, where he attended Friends Central, a local Quaker
school. Demonstrating an early interest in science, he early
won an award for a computer that he designed and built.

In the late 1950s, while majoring in Physics at New
York's Columbia University, De Palma began to produce and
direct a series of short films--among them ICARUS and
660124, THE STORY OF AN IBM CARD. WOTON'S WAKE,
a short satire on silent films, won for De Palma the 1963
Rosenthal Foundation Award, with the prize committee noting
that De Palma's talent is "unusually joyful as well as satirical."

De Palma enrolled in Sarah Lawrence College for
graduate work in Theatre Arts; he received his M. A. in
1964. His first feature film, THE WEDDING PARTY, was
produced during his graduate study. The film, co-produced
with his teacher, Wilfred Leach, was completed in 1963, although it was only released in April 1969, after the success
of De Palma's third film, GREETINGS. De Palma's second
feature, MURDER A LA MOD, was released soon afterward.
His split-screen version of the play DIONYSUS IN 69 (one
side of the screen featured the actors; the other, the audience) opened on March 20, 1970.

After the completion of his first commercially-produced

139

film, GET TO KNOW YOUR RABBIT (1972), De Palma was
in a position to buy back from Filmways Pictures a number
of his projects, including SISTERS, PHANTOM OF THE PAR-
ADISE, and HOME MOVIES (the latter eventually produced on
the campus of Sarah Lawrence College). He has since successfully worked in an impressive number of genres, including suspense, comedy, political thriller. Mr. De Palma is
married to actress Nancy Allen. He is presently in production with the Oliver Stone-scripted SCARFACE, starring Al
Pacino.

Note: Although three films in this filmography--THE WED-
DING PARTY, MURDER A LA MOD, and DIONYSUS IN 69--
are not available for commercial viewing, information on
them is provided for the sake of completeness.

THE WEDDING PARTY (1963)

Direction and Script: Brian De Palma, Wilfred Leach, Cyn-
   thia Munroe
Cinematography: Peter Powell
Editing: Brian De Palma
Sound: Betsy Taylor
Music: John Herbert McDowell
Mixing: Jim Townsend
Costumes: Ellen Rand
Produced by Brian De Palma, Wilfred Leach, and Cynthia
   Munroe for Ondine Productions.
Released by Powell Productions Plus.
Running Time: 90 minutes.

Cast: Jill Clayburgh (the bride), Valda Setterfield (Mrs.
Fish), Charles Pfluger (the groom), Jennifer Salt (Phoebe),
Robert De Niro (Cecil), John Braswell (Reverend Oldfield),
Raymond McNally (Mr. Fish), Sue Ann Converse (Nanny),
William Finley (Alistair), Judy Thomas (organist), Klaus
Kollmar, Jr. (Jean-Claude/Klaus/Hindu).

Synopsis: A satire on weddings and the social rites attendant with them.

MURDER A LA MOD (1968)

Direction: Brian De Palma
Script: Brian De Palma
Cinematography: Jack Harrell
Editing: Brian De Palma
Sound: Robert Fiore
Music: John Herbert McDowell
Produced by Ken Burrows. Released by Aries Documentaries.
Running Time: 80 minutes.

Cast: Andra Akers (Tracy), William Finley (Otto), Margo Norton (Karen), Jared Martin (Christopher), Ken Burrows (Wiley), Lorenzo Catlett (policeman), Jennifer Salt, Laura Stevenson, Kaura Rubin, Melanie Mander.

Synopsis: Murder, seen from three different viewpoints.

GREETINGS (1968)

Direction: Brian De Palma
Script: Charles Hirsch, Brian De Palma
Cinematography: Robert Fiore
Editing: Brian De Palma
Sound: Charles Ritts, Jeffrey Lesser
Music: The Children of Paradise
Costumes: Chuck Shields (pseudonym for Charles Hirsch)
Produced by Charles Hirsch for West End Film; released by Sigma III. Rated X.
Running Time: 88 minutes.

Cast: Robert De Niro (Jon Rubin), Jonathan Worden (Paul Shaw), Gerrit Graham (Lloyd Clay), Allen Garfield (porno merchant), Ted Lescault (bookstore manager), Tisa Chiang (Vietnamese girl), Jack Cowley (photographer), Bettina Kugel (Tina), Megan McCormick (Marina), Richard Landis (ex-GI), Ray Tuttle (television news correspondent), Ashley Oliver (Bronx secretary).

Synopsis: Two friends of draft age try to help out a third friend when he is ordered to report for his Army physical

by keeping him up all night, encouraging him to dupe the
examining officer, etc. GREETINGS is laced with loosely
connected bits and pieces of comic business, although the
film also contains a sub-text about one of the friends' fascination with the John F. Kennedy assassination that lends
an appropriately morbid tone to the proceedings.

DIONYSUS IN 69 (1970)

Direction: Brian De Palma, assisted by Bruce Rubin, Robert
   Fiore
Script: (DIONYSUS IN 69 is a documentary film of the play
   by Richard Schechner)
Cinematography: Robert Fiore, Brian De Palma
Editing: Brian De Palma, Bruce Rubin
Sound: Bruce Rubin
Mixing: Jim Townsend
Produced by Brian De Palma, Robert Fiore, Bruce Rubin.
   Rated X.
Running Time: 90 minutes.

Cast: The Performance Group: Remi Barclay, Samuel Blaz-
er, John Bosseau, Richard Dic, William Finley, Joan MacIn-
tosh, Vickie May, Patrick McDermott, Margaret Ryan, Richard Schechner, William Shephard, Ciel Smith.

Synopsis: A split-screen filmed version of the play, as performed by The Performance Group.

HI, MOM (1970)

Direction: Brian De Palma
Script: Brian De Palma, adapted from a story by Charles
   Hirsch and Brian De Palma
Cinematography: Robert Elfstrom
Editing: Paul Hirsch
Music: Eric Kaz
Art Direction: Peter Bocour
Produced by Charles Hirsch for Sigma III.
Running Time: 87 minutes.

Cast: Robert De Niro (Jon Rubin), Allen Garfield (Joe Banner), Jennifer Salt (Judy Bishop), Lara Parker (Jeannie Mitchell), Gerrit Graham (Gerrit Wood), Charles Durning (apartment house superintendent), Peter Maloney (pharmacist), Floyd

Peterson (newscaster). Be Black, Baby troupe: Buddy But-
ler, David Connell, Milton Earl Forrest, Carolyn Craven,
Joyce Griffin, Kirk Kerksey. Be Black, Baby audience:
Ruth Alda, Beth Bowden, Gene Elman, Joe Fields, Paul
Milvy, Joe Stillman, Carol Vogel.

Synopsis: The Robert De Niro character from GREETINGS
returns, this time fully intent on making a film about his
neighbors across the alley from his run-down apartment
house. De Niro's gradual radicalization is shown to be simultaneous with friend Gerrit Graham's increasing involvement with a theatre troupe, which De Niro eventually joins.
HI, MOM's last reel is comprised of the troupe's performance of their confrontation play, Be Black, Baby.

GET TO KNOW YOUR RABBIT (1972)

Direction: Brian De Palma
Script: Jordan Crittenden
Cinematography: John Alonzo
Editing: Peter Colbert
Sound: Robert Miller
Music: Jack Elliott
Art Direction: William Malley
Magic Adviser: H. Blackstone, Jr.
Produced by Paul Gaer and Steve Bernhardt. Associate Pro-
    ducer: Robert Birnbaum. Released by Warner Bros.
Running Time: 93 minutes.

Cast: Tom Smothers (Donald Beeman), John Astin (Mr. Turnbull), Katharine Ross (The Terrific-Looking Girl), Orson
Welles (Mr. Delasandro), Allen Garfield (Vic), Hope Summers (Mrs. Beeman), M. Emmet Walsh (Mr. Wendel), Su-
zanne Zenor (Paula), Samantha Jones (Susan), Jack Collins
(Mr. Reese), Helen Page Camp (Mrs. Wendel), Charles Lane
(Mr. Beeman).

Synopsis: Donald Beeman, a frustrated employee working for
a large corporation headed by Mr. Turnbull, decides to aban-
don his job and his wife and become an itinerant tap-dancing
magician. After a modicum of success, his freedom is
spoiled by his former boss (now an unemployed alcoholic),
who turns the tap-dancing magician idea into a programmed,
soft-sell diversion for executives. Back where he started,
Donald escapes by making himself disappear.

SISTERS (1973)

Direction: Brian De Palma
Script: Brian De Palma and Louisa Rose, from De Palma's
  story
Cinematography: Gregory Sandor
Editing: Paul Hirsch
Sound: Russell Arthur
Music: Bernard Herrmann
Production Design: Gary Weist
Assistant Director: Ann Hopkins
Produced by Edward Pressman for Pressman-Williams. Re-
  leased by American International Pictures.
Running Time: 93 minutes.

Cast: Margot Kidder (Danielle/Dominique), Jennifer Salt
(Grace Collier), Charles Durning (Joseph Larch), William
Finley (Dr. Emil Breton), Lisle Wilson (Philip Wood), Dolph
Sweet (detective), Mary Davenport (Mrs. Collier), Barnard
Hughes (magazine editor).

Synopsis: An apparently innocent young woman, Danielle,
takes on the persona of her dead homicidal Siamese twin
whenever she is threatened by men. Her neighbor, Grace
Collier, sees Danielle murder a man and calls in the police,
with little success. Grace investigates Danielle on her own
and, with the dubious aid of a private detective, eventually
tracks Danielle down to the clinic where she used to live,
confronting both the girl and her doctor ex-husband at the
point of the final, albeit indecisive, revelation.

THE PHANTOM OF THE PARADISE (1974)

Direction: Brian De Palma
Script: Brian De Palma
Cinematography: Larry Pizer
Production Design: Jack Fisk
Editing: Paul Hirsch
Sound Editor: Dan Sable
Sound Mixing: Al Grammaglia, Magno Sound Inc.
Music: Paul Williams
Production Design: Jack Fisk
Music Supervision: Michael Arciaga, Jules Chaikin
Special Effects: Greg Auer
Produced by Edward Pressman for Pressman-Williams. Re-
  leased by Twentieth Century-Fox.
Running Time: 91 minutes.

Cast: William Finley (Winslow/the Phantom), Paul Williams
(Swan), Jessica Harper (Phoenix), Gerrit Graham (Beef), George
Memmoli (Philbin), Jeffrey Comanor, Archie Hahn, Harold
Oblong (The Juicy Fruits, The Undead, The Beach Bums),
Harry Calvert (night watchman), Gene Gross (Warden), Ken
Carpenter, Sam Forney (stage hands), Leslie Brewer, Celia
Derr, Linda Larimer, Roseanne Romine (surfgirls), Nydia
Amagas, Sara Ballantine, Kristi Bird, Cathy Buttner, Linda
Cox, Jane Deford, Bibi Hanen, Robin Jeep, Deen Summers,
Judy Washington, Susan Weiswe (dancers), Janet and Jean
Savarino (singing twins), Sandy Catton and Friends (Black
singers), Nancy Moses, Diana Walden (back-up singers),
William Donovan, Scott Lane, Dennis Olivieri, Adam Wade
(reporters), Andrew Epper, Jim Lovelett (doubles for Wins-
low), James Gambino, Steven Richmond (doubles for Swan).

Synopsis: A composer, Winslow, brings his rock opera to
Swan, the head of Death Records, who steals the music and
disfigures and imprisons the young man. Winslow swears to
revenge himself against Swan and recapture the young singer
he loves, Phoenix. A rock-opera update of the Lon Chaney
original.

OBSESSION (1976)

Direction: Brian De Palma
Script: Paul Schrader; story by Schrader and De Palma
Cinematography: Vilmos Zsigmond
Editing: Paul Hirsch
Sound Editor: Dan Sable
Sound Mixer: David Ronne
Music: Bernard Herrmann, performed by The National Phil-
harmonic and The Thames Choir
Art Direction: Jack Senter
Visual Consultant: Anne Pritchard
Portrait Paintings: Barton De Palma
Produced by George Litto and Harry Blum. A George Litto
Production. Released by Columbia.
Executive Producer: Robert S. Bremson.
Running Time: 98 minutes.

Cast: Cliff Robertson (Michael Courtland), Genevieve Bujold
(Elizabeth Courtland/Sandra Portinari), John Lithgow (Robert
La Salle), Wanda Blackman (Amy Courtland), Sylvia Williams
(Judy), Patrick McNamara (kidnapper), Stanley J. Reyes (In-
spector Brie), Stocker Fontelieu (Dr. Ellman), Nella Simoncini

Barbieri (Mrs. Portinari), Tom Felleghy (Italian businessman), Don Hood (Ferguson), Regis Cordic (newscaster), John
Creamer (Justice of the Peace), Thomas Carr (paper boy),
Fain M. Gogrove (secretary), Andrea Esterhazy (D. Annun-
zio), Loraine Despres (Jane), Clyde Ventura (ticket agent).

Synopsis: The kidnapped wife and daughter of Michael Courtland, a successful New Orleans businessman, appear to die
in an auto accident after the ransom they were being held for
is not paid.   Years later Courtland, traveling in Italy with
his partner, Robert La Salle, meets a young girl who appears to be his dead wife's double.   He courts and wins her,
although on his return home he learns that she is really his
grown-up daughter, who escaped her mother's conflagrant end,
and who has now, at La Salle's behest, sworn to avenge herself against her father.   All is resolved at the end: Michael
kills La Salle; daughter and father are reunited.

CARRIE (1976)

Direction: Brian De Palma
Script: Lawrence D. Cohen, based on the novel by Stephen
    King
Cinematography: Mario Tosi
Art Direction: Jack Fisk, William Kenny
Editing: Paul Hirsch
Sound Editing: Dan Sable
Sound Mixing: Bertil Jalberg
Music: Pino Donaggio
Art Direction: William Kenny, Jack Fisk
Special Effects: Gregory M. Auer
Stunt Coordinator: Richard Weiker
Costumes: Rosanna Norton
Produced by Paul Monash.   Released by United Artists.   As-
    sociate Producer: Louis Stroller.
Running Time: 98 minutes.

Cast: Sissy Spacek (Carrie White), Piper Laurie (Margaret
White), Amy Irving (Sue Snell), William Katt (Tommy Ross),
John Travolta (Billy Nolan), Nancy Allen (Chris Hargenson),
Betty Buckley (Miss Collins), P.J. Soles (Norma Watson),
Sydney Lassick (Mr. Fromm), Stefan Gierash (Mr. Morton),
Priscilla Pointer (Mrs. Snell), Michael Talbot (Freddy), Doug
Cox (class photographer--The Beak), Harry Gold (George),
Noelle North (Frieda), Cindy Daly (Cora), Edie McGlurg
(Helen), Rory Stevens (Kenny), Anson Downes (Ernest), Dier-

dre Berthrong (Rhonda), Cameron De Palma (boy on bicycle).

Synopsis: Carrie--a shy, withdrawn high school girl--acquires telekinetic powers, which she uses to escape from the oppression of her evangelist mother and which she eventually unleashes on her classmates at the Senior Prom after two of her "enemies" publicly disgrace her. Carrie returns home, her mother attempts to kill "the witch," and both die in their telekinetically-collapsed house.

THE FURY (1978)

Direction: Brian De Palma
Script: John Farris
Cinematography: Richard H. Kline
Editing: Paul Hirsch
Sound Editing: Dan Sable
Music: John Williams
Art Direction: Richard Lawrence
Production Design: Bill Malley
Special Effects: A. D. Flowers
Costumes: Theoni V. Aldredge
Produced by Frank Yablans for Frank Yablans Presentations, Inc. Released by Twentieth Century-Fox. Executive Producer: Ron Preissman. Associate Producer: Jack B. Bernstein.
Running Time: 118 minutes.

Cast: Kirk Douglas (Peter Sandza), John Cassavetes (Childress), Carrie Snodgrass (Hester), Amy Irving (Gillian), Charles Durning (Dr. Jim McKeever), Andrew Stevens (Robin), Fiona Lewis (Susan Charles), Carol Rossen (Dr. Ellen Lindstrom), Joyce Easton (Mrs. Bellaver), William Finley (Raymond), Jane Lambert (Vivian Nuckells), Rutanya Alda (Kristen), Sam Laws (Blackfish), Alice Nunn (Mrs. Callahan), J. Patrick McNamara (Robertson), Melody Thomas (LaRue), Hilary Thompson (Cheryl), J. P. Bumstead (Greene), Patrick Billingsley (Lander), Dennis Franz (Bob), Barry Cullison (driver in first chase), Anthony Hawkins (shotgun in first chase), Albert Stevens (Arab Prince), Gordon Jump (Nuckells), Eleanor Merriam (Mother Nuckells), Harold Johnson (garbage man), Mickey Gilbert, Hanns Manship, Marland Proctor (CIA agents), Michael Copeland, Alfred Tinsley (young tough guys), Laura Innes (Jody), Clair Nelson (Dr. Becker), Al Wyatt (security driver), Peter O'Connell (Dr.

Conn), Daryl Hannah (Pam), Wayne Dahmer (Nelson), Tom
Blair (Top Guy #1), Gunnar Lewis (Top Guy #2), Marshall
Colt, Stephen Johnson, Robin Marmor, Roberta Feldner (tech-
nicians).

Synopsis: A telekinetic youngster is kidnapped from his father
by a defecting agent. The father, with the aid of a psychically-
gifted girl, goes in search of both his son and his kidnapper.
All meet in the end at the agent's country house, where violent, albeit deserved ends, await virtually everyone.

HOME MOVIES (1980)

Direction: Brian De Palma
Script: Robert Harders, Gloria Norris, Kim Ambler, Dana
    Edelman, Stephen Lemay, Charles Loventhal, from a story
    by Brian De Palma
Cinematography: James L. Carter
Editing: Corky O'Hara
Editorial Supervision: Paul Hirsch
Sound: Rick Wadell
Music: Pino Donaggio; conducted by Natale Massara
Art Direction: Tom Surgal
Animated Titles: Howard Danelowitz
Produced by Brian De Palma, Jack Temchin, and Gil Adler
    for SLC Films. Released by United Artists. Associate
    Producers: Sam L. Irvin, Jr., Mark Rosman
Running Time: 90 minutes.

Cast: Kirk Douglas (Dr. Tuttle, The Maestro), Nancy Allen
(Kristina), Keith Gordon (Dennis), Gerrit Graham (James),
Vincent Gardenia (Dr. Byrd), Mary Davenport (Mrs. Byrd),
Captain Haggerty (Officer Quinn), Loretta Tupper (Grandma),
Theresa Saldana (Judy), Kari Borg (Swedish Nurse), Kim
Herbert (Biker), Stephen Le May (Matthew), Ross Barnes
(Mark), Charles Loventhal (Thomas), Jeff Graham (Luke),
Robert Micklas (Andrew), Erin Lynch (Little Girl), Jon Daw-
son (Uncle Nelson), Colter Rhule (wise guy in class), Symie
Dahut (stripper), Al MacLennon (waiter), Tom Surgal (student
holding sign), Bunny (Bunny).

Synopsis: A light, comic pastiche. The Byrd family (Momma, Doctor Poppa, and son Dennis) is visited by eldest son
James, who brings along his bride-to-be, Christina. James'
unstructured teaching methods at the college combine with
Dennis' pathetic efforts in his Maestro-taught Star Therapy

film course to produce great humor. Christina, too, joins
the act, as she is revealed to be not only James' intended,
but also a cafe entertainer whose scatologically-minded pup-
pet, Bunny, seems to have a voice and will of his own.

DRESSED TO KILL (1980)

Direction: Brian De Palma
Script: Brian De Palma
Cinematography: Ralf Bode
Editing: Jerry Greenburg
Sound Mixer: John Bolz
Music: Pino Donaggio; conducted by Natale Massara
Production Designer: Gary Weist
Costumes: Ann Roth
Costume Designer: Gary Jones
Produced by George Litto for Cinema 77 Films. Released
    by Filmways Pictures. Associate Producer: Fred Caruso.
    Rating: R.
Running Time: 105 minutes.

Cast: Michael Caine (Dr. Robert Elliott), Angie Dickinson
(Kate Miller), Nancy Allen (Liz Blake), Keith Gordon (Peter
Miller), Dennis Franz (Detective Marino), David Margulies
(Dr. Levy), Ken Baker (Warren Lockman), Brandon Maggart
(Cleveland Sam), Susanna Clemm (Bobbi), Fred Weber (Mike
Miller), Sean O'Rinn (museum cabbie), Bill Randolph (chase
cabbie), Robert Lee Rush (hood #1), Mary Davenport (woman
in coffee shop).

Synopsis: A married woman with masochistically-tainted
erotic fantasies gets her wish when, after a brief fling with
a man she picks up in a museum, she is slashed to death in
an elevator by a mysteriously garbed blonde. A female witness to the murder, along with the victim's son, eventually
identify the real killer: the woman's psychiatrist.

BLOW OUT (1981)

Direction: Brian De Palma
Script: Brian De Palma
Cinematography: Vilmos Zsigmond
Editing: Paul Hirsch
Sound Mixer (Dolby Stereo): Jim Tannenbaum
Music: Pino Donaggio; conducted by Natale Massara

Production Designer: Paul Sylbert
Set Designer: Jeannine Oppewall
Underwater Cameraman: Rex Metz
Costume Designer: Vicki Sanchez
Produced by George Litto for Cinema 77/Geria Films. Re-
    leased by Filmways Pictures. Executive Producer/Pro-
    duction Manager: Fred Caruso.
Running Time: 107 minutes.

Cast: John Travolta (Jack Terri), Nancy Allen (Sally Bedina),
John Lithgow (Burke), Dennis Franz (Manny Karp), Peter Boy-
den (Sam), Curt May (Frank Donohue), Ernest McClure (Jim),
Dave Roberts (Anchor Man #1), Maurice Copeland (Jack Man-
ners), Claire Carter (Anchor Woman), John Aquino (Detective), John Hoffmeister (McRyan), Patrick McNamara (Officer
Nelson), Terrence Currier (Lawrence Henry), Tom McCarthy
(policeman), Dean Bennett (Campus Guard).

Synopsis: Jack, a motion picture sound man, accidentally
records the sounds of a car crash in which a leading presidential candidate dies. Through an examination of his tape
and close scrutiny of photos of the crash, he ascertains that
the candidate was deliberately murdered. Aided by Sally, a
woman who was in the candidate's car but was saved by Jack,
Jack eventually discovers and kills the murderer, although
not in time to save Sally from meeting the same fate (and
at the same hands) as the candidate.

SCARFACE (1983)

An updating of the 1932 Howard Hawks film. Starring Al
Pacino.

The American Nightmare. Toronto: Festival of Festivals, 1979. Contains Robin Wood's psycho-sexual interpretation of SISTERS and articles with similar critical approaches on films like NIGHT OF THE LIVING DEAD, MARTIN, ASSAULT ON PRECINCT 13, etc. The mythic elements brought out in the critiques of the Romero and Carpenter films bear closer study.

Anobile, Richard, ed. Psycho. New York: Avon Books, 1974. Now out-of-print, this stills-dominated version of the Hitchcock film, complete with the dialogue (which, through a copy error, is transposed on pages 80-81), remains the best non-audio-visual source for an unhurried study of this major work.

Cinefantastique. An excellent magazine with thoughtful, intelligent, insightful articles on fantasy films. Photo layouts are always of superb quality. The following issues contain articles on De Palma's work:
    4-2. Cover story on PHANTOM OF THE PARADISE ("De Palma of the Paradise").
    6-1. De Palma and Sissy Spacek on the filming of CARRIE.
    6-4/7-1; 7-2. Articles on the filming of THE FURY and coverage of location shooting in Chicago.

De Palma, Brian. Blow Out. New York: Bantam Books, 1981.

_____, with Campbell Black. <u>Dressed to Kill</u>. New York:
Bantam Books, 1980.
   Trade paperback versions of the films.

Gelmis, Joseph. <u>The Film Director As Superstar</u>. New
   York: Doubleday, 1970. Contains an informative interview with De Palma and Charles Hirsch conducted soon
   after the successful opening of GREETINGS.

Kael, Pauline. <u>Reeling</u>. New York: Warner Books, 1975.
   Contains a perceptive review of PHANTOM OF THE PAR-
   ADISE and an abrupt dismissal of SISTERS.

_____. <u>When the Lights Go Down</u>. New York: Holt,
Rinehart, and Winston, 1980. Excellent reviews of CAR-
RIE and THE FURY.

_____. Review of DRESSED TO KILL. <u>The New Yorker</u>,
August 4, 1980.

_____. Review of BLOW OUT. <u>The New Yorker</u>, July
27, 1981.

King, Stephen. <u>Carrie</u>. New York: Doubleday, 1974. Interesting as a contrast to the Lawrence D. Cohen screen-
   play approach to the story.

La Valley, Albert J., ed. <u>Focus on Hitchcock</u>. New York:
   Prentice-Hall, 1972. Excellent essays on Hitchcock's
   work, including Raymond Durgnat's fine piece on PSYCHO.

Monaco, James. <u>American Film Now</u>. New York: New
   American Library, 1979. The section on De Palma contains interesting, albeit short comments on the director's
   films. The book contains a copious filmography.

<u>Monthly Film Bulletin</u>, published by The British Film Insti-
   tute. Detailed, albeit usually negative reviews of De Palma's work.
      1974, p. 121, SISTERS (released in Great Britain as
         BLOOD SISTERS).
      1975, p. 112, PHANTOM OF THE PARADISE.
      1976, p. 217, OBSESSION.
      1977, p. 3, CARRIE.
      1978, p. 200, THE FURY.
      1979, p. 174, HI, MOM.

Spoto, Donald. The Art of Alfred Hitchcock. New York:
    Hopkinson and Blake, 1976. An indispensable critical ap-
    proach to the great director's films.